Foreword 2
The beginning of time, at least as far as I'm concerned 3
The Salad Days 12
Characters from the '40s and '50s 17
Production in the Early Days 23
Convention, Advertising, and College 34
The Coosa Queen, Engagement to Anne, Dalton 42
Dalton 46
Carrollton and Competition 51
The 1950s and '60s 57
Cedartown 66
Cartersville 67
Valdosta 72
Harvard, Unions 76
The 1970s 80
The New Rome Plant 91
Intrabrand Competition Act, Consolidation and Saccharine Ban 97
Soft Drink Associations 102
The 1980s 108
The Decision to Sell 115
My Service in the Navy 129
My Experience in Civic Affairs 146
Potpourri 180
Afterward 202
3rd Afterward 203
Memorandum of Thanks 204

Foreword

These memoirs represent a sincere attempt to describe my life, my career, and the much forgotten early days of the Coca-Cola industry. I hope that my grandchildren, and perhaps even their children, will read these words one day and gain some sense of whence they came.

While a person can become very much involved in business—perhaps even selfishly so—there exists another option to balance one's time by contributing to the community, the state, and the world in which one lives. If my words inspire any, all, or just one of these ends, my goal will have been achieved.

As you read this document, you will noticed the word "I" is used way too much. But since this is a book about my life, I don't see any other way to do it. However, "I" apologize in advance.

-Frank Barron, February 2001

The beginning of time, at least as far as I'm concerned

My name is William Franklin Barron, Jr., and I was born in Rome, Georgia on December 31, 1931.

I have records of the Barron family going back to 1741, when the first William Barron arrived in Augusta from Waterford, Ireland. The family started many years earlier, though, in a small Irish town of Burnchurch near Kilkenny Island. In those days the family went by name "Fitzgerald."

My father was William Franklin Barron, Sr. His father, in turn, was Frank Smith Barron, or "FS." FS was born in Carrollton, Georgia in about 1870. He lived most of his life in Rome, although I do remember having heard that he lived for a brief time in Chatooga County. I don't know a great deal about his background, except that he came to Rome sometime in the late 1800's—probably around 1895.

FS met and wooed Minnie Lee Sharpe, whose maiden name was actually Cooper. She had been the daughter of Mr. Cooper, a riverboat captain who plied the Coosa River. I can remember my Uncle Alfred Lee telling me many times with great bitterness how Mr. Cooper abandoned Minnie Lee, her mother, and her sister Nettie. He ran off with a riverboat girl, or some such escapade. Later, Minnie Lee's mother was married to a Mr. Sharpe and they had one daughter, Will, who later married a Brisendine. That story has to do with a Fort Valley relationship that I will share later. The other sister was named Nettie, and she married a Mr. Bailey from North Carolina. Nettie has no great part to this story except that I remember her very well.

FS and Minnie Lee, or "Money" as we affectionately called her (I assume because "Minnie" had been too hard to pronounce), had three children: WF, my father, who was born in 1898; Kathleen Virginia Barron, born about 1904; and Alfred Lee Barron, born in 1908. Kathleen, or "Aunt Katty," married a Canadian and lived in Canada most of her life. She figures prominently in the sale of the company, so I will return to her later. My uncle, Alfred Lee, eventually ran the business in connection with my father and my grandfather.

The story of how FS originally got into the Coca-Cola Business is not overly clear in my mind. I know that he had been in the grocery store business, or so the popular tale went. He eventually went out of business (or "went broke," as we used to call it) twice in the grocery store business before he became involved with Coca-Cola.

Coca-Cola has been in business since 1885 as a fountain drink dispensed in soda fountains. In the beginning, there was very little –if any—idea that bottling would be successful. Mr. Whitehead and Mr. Lupton, two entrepreneurs from Chattanooga, went down to the Coca-Cola Company in Atlanta and asked for the rights to bottle from Mr. Asa Candler, who had bought the rights to the Coca-Cola formula from Dr. Pemberton, the syrup's inventor. Mr. Whitehead and Mr. Lupton got the rights to bottle pretty much all over the United States, with the exception of some obscure places such as New England, Mississippi and a few other discrete places.

It became apparent to these two entrepreneurs fairly quickly that they did not have enough money to build all the Coca-Cola plants for this fast growing product, so they came up with the idea of issuing exclusive franchises. The early franchises were basically non-terminable by the company. Bottlers were told to do the best they could. Of course, such vague instructions were subject to all sorts of interpretations.

I'm not going to spend a lot of time on the history of Coca-Cola because that's recounted far better by others, in other places. I'll suffice it to say that the early Coca-Cola bottling plants were in Chattanooga and Atlanta, which, of course, were in relatively close proximity to Rome. I suspect that the Coca-Cola's sold in my grandfather's store came from Chattanooga.

I have memories of being told that my grandfather used to go down to the train station to pick up Coca-Cola's for his grocery store. Of course, the bottles then were all returnable. In those days, no one had ever heard of charging a deposit because the supposition was that people were honest. If they bought ten cases of Coca-Cola's, then they would bring ten cases worth of empty bottles back to be refilled. That was the procedure, until about the mid 1970's when non-returnables began to be a major factor.

On January 10, 1901, FS officially received the Coca-Cola franchise. (The original balance sheet, dated the very same day, is currently in the possession of Alfred Lee's children, Mike and Al.) We know that prior to the end of 1900, there were only five Coca-Cola plants, and that by the end of 1901, there were only nine. Thus, four Coca-Cola bottling plants were started in 1901. Since it would be logical to presume that not many plants were started before January 10, we feel safe in assuming that F.S.'s franchise, the Rome Coca-Cola Bottling Plant, is probably the sixth oldest franchise in the world.

There is reason to suspect that F.S. was unable to pay for the franchise at the time of its purchase in 1901. As was very common in those days, the Whiteheads and the Luptons would retain for example, five percent of the stock in the company. As the franchise prospered, they would receive dividends in order to get their money back. Because little is known about Coca-Cola operations in the early days, I do not know how successful the bottled product was at first. Documentation exists that would indicate that by 1910 my grandfather was fairly successful.

I do not know exactly where my grandfather lived in those early days, although I do know that his home was on Avenue A in Rome. His street ran parallel to the street that is now Martha Berry Boulevard, and his house sat behind what is now a housing project in an area called "Fourth Ward". My grandfather lived in that home for a good many years. Then, sometime between 1908 and 1910, he built a house on 2nd Avenue. Still standing today, the house is owned by an accounting firm named the Rand Group. Joel Jones is the principle of that group, and as far as I know the group is currently operating from that house. The building is fairly large and prestigious in appearance, so my guess is that my grandfather was doing pretty well by the time he built it.

I remember little anecdotal things about my grandfather, such as how he was a member of the Rotary Club and that he loved to trade cars and horses. One day, he was sitting in front of a building that he owned on 5th Avenue which is where 5th Avenue Drug Store was located, later became 5th Avenue Drugstore talking to some of his friends, and they all noticed a car was sitting nearby with some liquid underneath it. The men began to discuss whether the liquid was water or gasoline. My grandfather was so convinced that the liquid was water that he said he was going to throw a match and see if the water lit. Well, it did. The car ignited into flames, and my grandfather had to buy it.

FS never went to college, but my father graduated from Washington & Lee University in Lexington, Virginia. It was about the time that World War I was in full bloom.

Willie in College

I seem to have heard of some connection between my father attending Washington & Lee and the influence of Ms. Lettie Pate Whitehead Evans. She was Mr. Whitehead's widow and thus extremely wealthy. Ms. Evans was the former Ms. McConkey, and she was born and lived in Natural Bridge, VA. There were two large estates left at her death. One of these was the Lettie Pate Evans Fund, which provides

Washington & Lee, Berry College and three other colleges with a huge income each year. Her other foundation, the Whitehead Foundation, provides scholarship money to Berry as well. I suspect that my grandfather's closeness to the then Mrs. Whitehead had something to do with my father attending Washington & Lee. Ms. Evans always said that Washington & Lee, the college of General Robert E. Lee, was great in the South in those days.

My father finished his courses at Washington & Lee in three years. I do know that he was discharged from the Army in 1918. He then came to Rome, Georgia to work with FS in the Coca-Cola business.

Somewhere along the line, my father and grandfather hooked up with a gentleman by the name of Mr. E. D. Cole from Cartersville, GA. I assume that Mr. Cole was well off financially, because he soon began to help my father and grandfather expand their holdings. Together the three men formed Carrollton Coca-Cola, Cedartown Coca-Cola, and Cartersville Coca-Cola. In the early days, these three plants were all in the same ownership. (That is to say that they were, practically speaking, one corporation, and in fact may have been.) It was only later, probably in the 1930's, that the three corporations were separated for income tax purposes.

Although he didn't realize it until afterwards, a very important event happened in the life of my father in 1920. Mary Sue Jones came to Rome from Commerce, Georgia. She was the daughter of the former Mildred Hardman and Gordon Taylor Jones. Mr. Jones, my Grandfather was from the state of Virginia. His Father had been an Assistant Treasurer Officer with the Confederacy during the Civil War. John Jones graduated from William and Mary in 1849 or thereabouts. Mary Sue came to attend Shorter College, which was then, as it remains now, a Baptist institution with a very close affiliation with the Georgia Baptist Convention. Mary Sue and my father met, eventually marrying in 1924 when she graduated from

Shorter. My sister, Virginia, was born in 1926 and I was born in 1931. We were both delivered in Harbin Hospital, Virginia by Dr. Will Harbin and me by his brother Robert.

A great recession hit right about the time I was born. (In fact, it may have very well been the reason I was born.) Dad said that one thing he learned during the ensuing Depression was that if a person had a nickel to buy either an apple or a Coca-Cola, he would buy a Coca-Cola. The purchase added a little bright spot to his day. My father believed that the Coca-Cola bottling company was immune to the Depression, and he believed that until the day he died. I rather suspect he was right. Even though in my time there have been some rather difficult financial times, such as in 1958 and 1974, we certainly did not go broke and we always had enough to eat.

My father and mother lived in the home on 2nd Avenue with FS and Money for the first couple years of their marriage. In 1928, my father built a house at 304 East 4th Avenue, where Judge Jimmy Dick Maddox lives today. That was where I grew up as a youngster. I can remember some isolated incidents from my childhood, such as the day Daddy brought home a new car—a Dodge. I can also remember being taken to the Coca-Cola plant on 5th Avenue and the times when certain visitors came to our home. One visit I remember in particular was a visit we received one day from Mr. Stuart Gould.

My knowledge of the Gould family goes as far back as an old gentleman named Fred Gould, a man who lived in Rome in the early 1900's. Fred Gould owned an orange drink bottling plant that was located somewhere near the old railroad depot at the south end of Broad Street. That building has since burned. This is very near the property where Southeastern Mills now stands. Fred had at least two sons that I recall—Stuart and Roddy, who subsequently played prominent roles in my life. Roddy's widow, Margaret, is still living.

Mr. Fred Gould sold his orange plant in the early 1900's. Coca-Cola was becoming a dominant drink on the scene, and the vast assortment of other products such as Royal Crown, Double Cola, and Pepsi made it difficult for independent orange plants as a breed to survive. Inevitably, Mr. Gould's his two sons Roddy and Stuart went into various facets of the soft drink business. Stuart's choice was to join a company called "Liquid Carbonic." It was a company that made bottling machines, and Coca-Cola Bottlers accounted for a large portion of their business. The syrup was put into the machine and then bottles were filled with a carbon dioxide/water mixture (the substance that gave the drinks their "fizz"). The Liquid Lo-Pressure Filler, as it was called in those days, was the bottling machine of choice by most bottlers. It was very well made and was fairly simple to operate. Stuart Gould sold them. Roddy subsequently went into business selling crowns. We bought quite a few crowns from Roddy.

Because of our bottling plant's obvious need for filler machinery, Stuart began to visit our home quite frequently. He became more than merely a business associate—Stuart Gould became a family friend. I can remember that when he came to Rome to call on our bottling plant, Stuart would come and eat supper with us. It was quite the ordinary and decent thing for us to do.

Stuart entered my life in a very specific way much later, although I had known him for years. It turned out that his daughter Phoebe went to the University of Georgia and was a very close friend of my wife's. We even went to her wedding! Phoebe married a fellow named Ed Forio, whose father was the first public affairs officer of the Coca-Cola Company. Ed Forio, Sr. was succeeded by Ovid Davis, of great fame, and occupied the first chair which was held until just recently held by one of my dearest friends, Earl Leonard, a Senior Vice President of the Coca-Cola

Company. Ovid and I were also very close as long as he lived.

The Salad Days

Many people referred to the days before World War II as the "salad days," and to me this expression was especially true. Life was great.

A particular memory I have of my grandfather is back from those days. The only time I really remember seeing him was when I had been given a little wind-up tank truck. It looked like a squashed rectangle at an angle, and it had little rubber feet. After being would up, the tank would climb over books, blocks, or anything I might put in its path. I thought it was the greatest toy that a fellow could ever have. I went to my grandfather's house one day to show it to him, and I can remember that we both got down on the floor together to watch my tank climb over books.

As for the rest of what I remember of my grandfather, I'm not sure if my memories are authentic ones or if they are memories I have recreated from photographs. I do remember that he was a very gentle man. He was a tall and spare with a little mustache. My memories of his wife, my grandmother, are very few. All that I seem to remember is that she was present often and that I knew who she was. Both my grandfather and my grandmother died in 1936 in a period of about six weeks. I was only five at the time, so it would be natural that I would have very little memory of them.

Of course, very prominent in my life in those days was my Uncle Alfred and his wife Jane. They had married in 1931, but when I was a boy they had no children yet. Uncle Alfred was ten years younger than my father, and he liked my sister and me very much. I have great memories of him picking us up on Sunday mornings to go swimming. Royce Peugh, who worked at the Coca-Cola plant, and was a great friend of all of ours, would usually come along. We would go down to the city swimming pool, located where the new civic building is now on West 2nd Street, which was then known as Tribune Street. Those were great days.

Royce Peugh is another individual worthy of mention. Royce probably spent his whole life, from the mid 1930's until he retired, working for the Rome Coca-Cola Bottling Company. The only break in his service to Coca-Cola was the time he served as a Chief Petty Officer in the Navy during World War II. He died in the fall of 1997 and was a great individual.

A great friend of Royce, my father, and Uncle Alfred in particular, was a man named Mark Horton. He was the sheriff. To have an uncle and a father who knew the sheriff was one of the most exciting things for a boy to imagine! He and my Uncle Alfred Lee were great horse fans. They would ride horse together on Sundays.

There are a few other people I remember from those days. I remember Oscar and Horton Gunn, two brothers who were both very mechanically inclined and geniuses in their field. At the plant, they ran mechanical operations, the purchase of machinery, and the machinery's installation. Another person I remember from those days is Bud West. Bud was a huge, mountain-sized man who had no hair on his head and the constant smell of cigars about his person. He was a good at simply everything. A native of Cedartown, Bud came from a very fine family. And then there was Mildred White. She was the do-it-all secretary. Mildred counted the money, answered the telephone, and tended to everyone. (As an interesting sideline, Bud and Mildred married in the late 1940's. She had divorced, and Bud's wife had passed away.) Mildred had a tragic situation in the late 1940's. Her only son, Billy White, accidentally killed himself with Bud's pistol. The gun went off and killed poor Billy.

It was very easy to travel from the house to the Coca-Cola plant on my bicycle. I was given my first bicycle—a green one—in 1943, when I was twelve. I remember very well riding my bicycle to the Coca-Cola plant in the early morning. At the plant, I would sort bottles until noon for $ .50 a day.

In the mid 1940's, I began high school. I was working at the Coca-Cola plant every summer, a tradition that would continue well into my college days. (I did, however, attend summer camp when I was 12 or 13.)

My summer schedules were very routine. Daddy would wake me up in the mornings at 5:30, and I would ride down to the plant with him. (When I became old enough to drive my own car, I drove myself.) After getting the trucks off on their routes, Daddy would come home again to eat breakfast at 7:00. During the winter, when I was in school, I would always get up in time to eat breakfast with my Daddy. He would eat breakfast and then go back to the Coca-Cola plant about 8:15 or 8:30. I have always been raised to get up at 5:30, go to work, unlock the door, and greet everybody as they came in. We stayed at the plant until the doors were locked at 6:00 or later in the afternoon, Monday through Saturday. I have often

Willie. FS and Me

been asked why I did not play golf or tennis, but my answer was always that I didn't have time for those things. It was no great burden, and I felt deprived of nothing. That's just the way life in the Coca-Cola business was.

When I was in the third grade, my teacher who as near as I recall, was Mrs. Penelope Ramey asked some of us what our Fathers did for a living. I allegedly stood up in class and said, "I don't know what he does for a living but I know what he says." When being asked what, I said, "He says, early to bed, early to rise, work like hell and advertise." I guess that sums up the Coca-Cola business in a few sentences and just a few words.

There's an interesting story which may or may not be true as to why the Barrons have always gotten up so early in the morning to go to work. My grandfather lived on 2nd Avenue, which was right on the trolley car line. The trolley would wake him up every morning at 5:30. When he woke up, he couldn't go back to sleep, so he would go to the plant. When my father came along, I suppose my grandfather decided that if he had to get up, then so did his son. When my time came, I got up too, and so did Frank III. The family has always gotten up at 5:30 or 5:15; I did it for thirty years. It became a way of life with us, and there were many good reasons for it. If the boss is there before a man arrives at work and after the man goes home, it's very difficult for him to complain that he is working harder than the boss. When my children came along, I came home for breakfast about two or three times per week, as my father before me had done. (Daddy had been able to come home every day because the Rome plant was located very close to where we lived. After we bought the Fort Valley and Valdosta plants, many of my mornings were spent in travel.) The trucks would need to be out on the road by 7:00 because certain businesses needed the Coca-Cola's delivered before their normal work crews arrived.

Therefore, our drivers would come in around approximately 6:45 to attend sales meetings. Everyone would get in their trucks, get the early delivery chore done, and then have their breakfast around 8:30 or 9:00. It was just our accepted way of doing things.

Characters from the '40s and '50s

I remember some real characters from my high school and early college days. There was a fellow named T'Tie Tolbert, whose job it was to deliver Coca-Cola's to the home market. T'Tie knew just about everybody in Rome. If there was a death in someone's family, he would take a little cooler of Coca-Cola's to the home so that the people coming by would have something cold to drink. He became the representative in charge of home delivery because his arm had been cut in a fight when he was a young man. He could only use one hand to carry things. T'Tie was a great American, and he was extremely kind to me when I was growing up.

Josh Redmond was a fellow who worked in Piedmont, Alabama for years and years. He never handled a case that I ever saw—that part was always done by his helper, Buster Hutchins. Buster had gone to work with Josh when he was about 12 or 13. Many years later, in the 1960's, he became a route salesman. By the time of his retirement he had become the senior salesman of the entire Rome organization. Buster's real name was Macon, but no one knew that for years and years. He was about as strong and stout as anyone I ever knew. I'll never forget one time when I was riding with Buster and I was trying very hard to do what I was supposed to do, helping to deliver the cases into the stores. But after two or three hours, Buster turned to me and said, "Mr. Frank, just get out of the way and let me do it!" Clearly, he could handle it by himself. I was just in the way.

There are so many other people I remember from Rome in those days, such as Clint Espy, E.K. Pope, the aforementioned Josh Redmond, Millard Fincher,

James Watters, and Charlie Floyd and others. Jerry Williams was an outstanding gentleman who later became a supervisor. He remains a friend to this day. I also have fond memories of Harlan Trotter, one of the funniest people I have ever known, and Guy Selman. Aubrey Jones, the plant's accountant, has also provided me with many warm and happy memories.

Frank Bramlett is a gentleman I remember from the refrigeration department. He was head of that department for years and years. Frank's grandmother, Cynthia Barron Bramlett, and my grandfather, Frank Barron, had been brother and sister. That makes him my second cousin. He was an outstanding gentleman who was with the company for many years.

I also remember gentlemen such as Mr. Watson, whose relatives still live in Rome; Millard Fincher, who became a supervisor; Tom House and Fred Coulter. Now there was a character if there ever was one.

Fred Coulter was little, a rooster sort of a fellow, with a very attractive personality. He stayed drunk a lot (although not when he was working), chased women, and had just about every other vice known to man. But he was one of the most amusing fellows I ever saw. During World War II, when our syrup was rationed and everything was on a very tight string, Fred had a team of horses and a little wagon that he loaded up with Coca-Cola's to sell up and down Broad Street. He worked Broad Street for 40 years or more. I remember as a child seeing Fred, those horses, and that old wagon.

I later worked the routes with Fred during the summers while I was in college. One of the things I remember most vividly about him is that he had an old Ford truck—a pre-World War II model—and boy, did he have that truck finely tuned. There are lots of interesting stories having to do with that truck of his. One of the interesting things he did was to make it move without ever being inside it. Over on 4th Avenue, in the lot across from where the old post office sits (where the parking deck is now), there was an old

Colonial store. The loading dock was located around back, so to get to it, the drivers had to go around to the back of the store and drive down into a pit. Fred would take his truck and back it down in there. He had the truck fixed so that if he put it in a certain gear, the truck would climb the hill, ever so slowly, without him in it. He even had it so that when he worked the stores on Broad Street (and we worked them all), he didn't have to double park his truck as he worked the stores. Fred would simply whistle, and the truck would follow him down the street! It was a very weird sight, and people would want to come around and ask him about how he got his truck to do that.

We worked every single store on Broad Street—perhaps it was because it was home to so many grocery stores. In fact, the beginning of Huffman-Salmon (later to become Piggly Wiggly) was on Broad Street. It was owned by Mr. Ed Salmon and Mr. Marvin Huffman. Mr. Huffman was Billy Huffman's daddy. Mr. Salmon later bought out Mr. Huffman and it then became the Piggly Wiggly store. In those days, Huffman-Salmon was THE store.

The Coca-Cola plant was located near Broad Street, on North 5th Avenue. Its street address was 106, 108 North 5th Avenue. Of course, I always found that address somewhat strange. It occupied about a fourth of a then city block, where the present, new civic building is located.

Walking in the front door of the Coca-Cola plant, one would see two offices fronted by a bit of glass and

a hallway. In the first office were two desks—one that belonged my uncle, Alfred Lee, and another one that belonged to my father. The next office housed Mildred West, the secretary. It also contained a stairway that led up to the second floor. In the back of Mildred's office was a large open space, about as big as

19

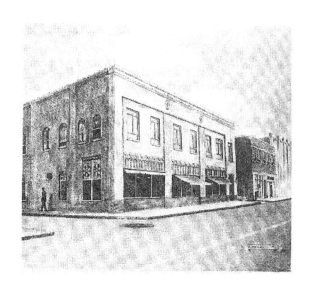

A drawing of the early Coca-Cola plant. We stayed in this building until 1977 when we moved out to the new plant on Hwy. 27 South

Rome Management Team Circa 1953

Walking straight down the hallway having come in the front door, facing away from the first two offices, one would come across the bottling room. The bottling room had one washer/filler type operation with open glass all the way around. A very popular diversion for young children was to come by the plant and head towards this room. Alfred, Willie, or Mildred would give them a little gift, such as a pencil, a blotter, or a tablet. The children were then allowed go in and watch the bottling operation, after which they would get a free Coca-Cola right off the line. When I would go, I would think, "Gosh, can I really take one and mix it up myself?" Even though my daddy owned the place and I was there often, it was still a thrilling event for me.

There are a lot of other people I remember from the early days of Coca-Cola production. I remember Ross Burns, who became manager of Gainesville, GA Coca-Cola and who came through our operation from time to time. Then there was Virginia Shiflett, or Ginny, who was our telephone operator. I suspect that Ginny knew just about everybody in Rome. If she didn't know them by their face, she at least knew them by their voice. When the phone at the plant would ring, and the person on the other end would say, "Ginny, let me speak to Willie," Ginny would answer, "Yes sir, Mr. Hardy." She knew them all by name, and they knew her. She was a great person. She left in the early 60's and went back to Shorter College to get a degree in teaching. She became a schoolteacher and is recently retired.

Another person I remember is Mule Fowler. Mr. Fowler became a supervisor with us, but he later left and got into the house moving business. Mule was a great salesman.

Production in the Early Days

To describe the bottling operation, I'll follow one empty case of 6 ½ ounce Coca-Cola bottles from the beginning to the end of the bottling process. In the beginning of the carbonated bottling business, beverages were pretty much put into any kind of bottle available. The bottles were sealed by a variety of different methodologies—probably even by pouring wax on top of the bottles at one point in time.

One of the earlier bottles was called the Hutcherson Bottle. This kind of bottle contained a little glass ball that was too large to go through the bottle's neck. Around the glass ball was a washer. As the bottle was filled, there was a little wire that could be yanked to seal the ball against the rim of the neck. The origination of the word "pop" came from the fact that when someone wanted to open the bottle, he or she would hit the wire and a "pop" sound would result as the gas escaped.

There are many stories running around about how unsanitary the first bottles were. A little space existed between the wire and the glass ball, and that was where the person drinking the beverage would put his or her mouth. According to the stories I've heard, it was common for horse manure to collect in these spaces. People drinking the beverages would just wipe off the opening, blow the bottle off, and keep right on drinking. I suppose that some of the consumers got diseases, but maybe folks then were of a heartier breed than they are now. Anyway, the industry did survive, and so did the people.

By 1915, it became apparent that there was a need for a distinctive bottle. It was becoming difficult for consumers to distinguish Coca-Cola bottles from the bottles of our competitors. A group called the Root

Glass Company, ancestors of our friend Chapman Root, was chosen for the job. (Chapman Root was the owner of the Orlando and Daytona Beach plants, among others.)

It is easy now to tell whether an old Coca-Cola bottle was produced prior to 1915 or post 1915 because the hobble skirt bottle didn't come into effect until 1915. The bottles made before 1915 were straight-sided and didn't have the name of where the product had been bottled. In those days, my grandfather would order a certain quantity of these bottles, and Chattanooga Glass Company (and perhaps other suppliers as well) would make them up. On the bottom of our straight sided bottles, some of which I have in my possession, there was a large "B" on the bottom that stood for the name Barron. Of course, mobility was not as great then, so bottles that were bottled in Rome probably stayed in Rome.

Having the name on the bottom on the bottle allowed us to create an interesting game. It was called "Far Away." We played this game in the plant as well as all over town. The way it was played was a person would get a bottle from a vending machine or even pull one out of a case. $.50 or $1.00 would be put up in a pot, and whoever got the bottle from the farthest away would win the pot.

When an empty 24 case of Coca-Cola bottles was brought in off the trucks, a procedure called "sorting bottles" occurred. Rome Coca-Cola, against the best wishes of the Coca-Cola Company, was an early seller of other products such as grapes, oranges, and other flavors. I remember in particular a strawberry flavored drink that we had. To me, the first three or four sips were pretty good, but that after that, it was the most terrible, awful tasting thing I had ever put in my mouth! In addition to the grape, orange, strawberry, and other flavors, we also bottled Buffalo Rock, which was somewhat of a ginger flavored product.

When the bottles came back from the trade, often times there were grape bottles or some of these other flavors mixed in with Coca-Cola bottles. An entry-level job was to sort through these bottles. The sorters had a method of lining up all the flats of bottles and going through them one by one. He would separate the bottles so that as they went into the bottling procedure, they were identified as either grape, Coca-Cola, or whatever. This completed the sorting procedure.

Once the bottles were sorted, they were brought to the end of a table that was part of a bottle washing machine. This giant piece of equipment was called the soaker. The bottles were placed individually on a moving conveyor. At the end of the conveyer, the bottles were turned over into a large, continuous chain that would carry the bottles through large tanks of hot, caustic soda and water. The result was that after soaking and rinsing, the bottles were totally and completely sanitary. Therefore, I know for a fact that the stories going around about mice ending up in Coca-Cola bottles are absolutely untrue. If a mouse were to be dropped into the tubs of caustic solution that our bottles were soaked through, there wouldn't be one scrap of that mouse left over—not even the bones.

After going through the soaker, the bottles would be ejected in spurts. One of the tricks we used was to keep a good bit of soap on the conveyers so that the bottles would move along smoothly. At the end of the soaker stood a lady dressed in clean, white, crisp clothes. She would watch to see that bottles did not fall over. One of the best of these ladies was a lady who has recently passed away. Her name was Anne Climer. During World War II, due to the shortage of men, Anne ran the filler. She was a marvelous person. If there were a bottle with a broken neck, Anne would remove it from the belt. If there happened to be a bottle with a chunk of tar on it, she would take that bottle to be re-washed or thrown away. She also had control of a big lever, which she could use to stop the whole machine in the event of a mechanical breakdown.

After the bottles had been through the soaker, they went on down the line for another six or eight feet to go through the filler. These were the same Liquid Low Pressure Fillers that Stuart Gould sold us back in the early days. Bottles went into a merry-go-round looking piece of equipment. There was a small one about three and four feet in diameter, and a larger one about seven or eight feet in diameter. These two carousels were attached to the same base. The purpose of the filler was to put exactly one ounce of syrup from the first carousel and carbonated water from the second carousel into each bottle. The carbonated water was, of course, refrigerated and pressurized, which kept the carbon dioxide in it. When a bottle got to the end of the carousel and was ready to be discharged, the pressure was relieved very slowly to keep the liquid from foaming. The syrup came down through pipes from a large tank, which was located upstairs in the syrup room. Open bottles coming from the second carousel were full with Coca-Cola and not foaming over. The bottles then went onto a very small carousel. There, what was known as the top, or crown, was placed on top. And that is how the bottles came to be filled and crowned.

Of course, at this point the Coca-Colas didn't appear the way you might expect—tasty, smooth mixtures of syrup and carbonation. No, instead, they looked rather funny. The brown, almost purplish-looking syrup had settled to the bottom of the bottle, and the top of the bottle was clear (or even yellowish) from the carbonated water that had gotten some syrup mixed up in it. Then the trick came—how could we mix up the Coca-Colas so that they would look like something folks might like to drink? What we did was to put the bottles in unique piece of equipment that looked a bit like a reading stand. Four holes were cut into it in the shape of upside down Coca-Cola bottles. There was a round table where the bottles accumulated after having been crowned, going round and round waiting to be pulled off the line. We would place them in the slots upside-down, whereupon a light would shine on them from underneath. The light allowed us to look through the Coca-Colas and see if any blocks, marbles, or foreign objects were in there. Occasionally there were, and we set those bottles aside. Once the Coca-Cola's were mixed up and checked for impurities, we would set them together in cases of 24. The cases were set in a pallet, or flat, which was drawn by a hand truck. (There were no forklift trucks in those days.) By pulling the bottles off of the accumulating table and turning them upside down to inspect them, the syrup and the carbonated water were mixed together sufficiently.

A bottling plant from the 40s and 50s

It was a matter of great pride among those who ran the accumulating table to see just how quickly the bottles could be mixed together and put into cases. There was a fellow named Junior Morgan who could keep up with the entire production line with one hand. He could pull two bottles, shake them, put them in a case, and keep the accumulating table empty all by himself. Sometimes, as a game, we would let the accumulating table fill completely full of bottles so that the bottles would begin backing up the conveyer line towards the filler and the crowner. Then, we would see how quickly we could clean off the table. (Keep in mind that the table was filling up at a rate of about 130 bottles per minute!) We had to take everything off the conveyer table, put the bottles in their cases, and then put the cases on the flats.

Perhaps here I should describe the methodology by which the cases moved through to the trucks. In those days, all of the trucks were loaded by hand. They consisted of a flat bed, some three or five beds high. The trucks all contained neat little rows of angle iron so that four cases would fit from one side of the truck to the other in great rows. There would be 10 or 12 rows, depending on how long the truck was and how far it had to go. When the cases came off the production line, they were arranged in flats. The flats were six cases long horizontally—six cases long by two wide on each level. Therefore, each level held twelve cases. On the fourth layer, we would lay three crossways and then two, two, and two, and then three crossways and then go up another layer. The purpose of all this cross-stacking was to give the cases some stability.

We had an extremely heavy metal hand truck that we rolled underneath and between the metal feet on the flat. We then leaned down very heavily, which raised the flat an inch or two off the ground and locked it in place so we could roll it. This was all done by hand. We had very stout young men (of whom I thought I was one) to do the pulling, lifting, and rolling. We kept the cases in rows so that we could keep track of our inventory and separate the cases by flavor. In later years, the different sizes of bottles came along, and the loading of the trucks became an enormously complex operation. In retrospect, it was reasonably simple in the early days.

Another important aspect of production was syrup delivery. Our syrups were delivered to us in big, metal drums made of stainless steel. Each drum held 55 gallons of syrup. The drums were delivered to us once a week, on Wednesdays, with an occasional second delivery being added later on in the week during the busy summer months. To unload the trucks, we had a ramp with finger-like protrusions that stuck up in the middle. These fingers were hydraulically loaded, so that when we pushed a drum off the truck and laid it on its round side, the drum would roll easily and safely. We had several people there to help during delivery time. Each person would grab a drum and roll it quickly. As always, there would be a lot of competition among us to see who could roll drums the fastest.

One of the best people at rolling the drums was a gentleman by the name of Alvin Carrol. Alvin came to work for us when he was sixteen, but he was already a stout young man. In later years, Alvin became a salesman, and subsequently, a supervisor. When he was in his forties, he left us and started the Alvin Carrol Service Station, where he remained until he died some years ago.

After the drums had been unloaded from the truck, we would take them to the back and count them. There they would sit until the time came for them to be used in production. However many drums were needed would be carried upstairs. Of course, there were a number of different methodologies that we used in getting the syrup out of the drums. Sometimes, we would pump the syrup into an open vat and make use of it that very day. Other times, we would pump the syrup into a large refrigerated tank to store the syrup for later use. The tank kept the syrup somewhere around 60 degrees, which assured there would be no loss of quality. One of the primitive methods of using a syrup drum was to line up several barrels and attach a small manifold at the end of the drum. The manifold was then attached to a pipe, which was connected directly to the syruper and the filler.

After the drums had been emptied of their syrup, we were naturally expected to return the empty drums to the delivery companies. The Coca-Cola Company always kept very close track of how many drums they had delivered to us. The stainless steel used to make the drums was quite expensive. If we ever were listed as having been delivered more drums of syrup than the number we returned, we were charged for the missing drums. As the wintertime came, we would cut back our inventory and return more drums than we received. Once a year, representatives from the company would come in and inventory our drums—just to make sure that we weren't selling them, or storing liquor in them, or doing anything else with the drums that they might consider to be inappropriate.

In later years, this entire system of unloading syrup drums from the truck, counting them, and pumping the syrup into tanks gave way to delivery by means of special trucks called syrup tank trucks. These were huge tankers full of syrup that could be pumped from outside the building directly into our refrigerated tanks. After this development, we didn't even have to be at the plant when syrup was delivered.

Another important factor in the syrup aspect of production was making the syrup for some of our flavored products. Our plant was probably one of the oldest NuGrape bottlers in the world at one point in time. In addition to NuGrape, we also bottled orange, strawberry, and other flavors. For the production of these flavored drinks, we didn't buy the syrup directly like we did for the Coca-Colas. The fun thing about the flavored products was that we bought only the concentrate, and then we got to make the syrup ourselves. To make the syrup from concentrate, we had to take great quantities of sugar, 100 pounds or so, and then throw the sugar into a huge tank filled with cold water. We used wooden paddles to stir the mixture until the sugar went into solution—that is, until we could let the mixture run between our forefingers and our thumbs without feeling any sugary grit. This was not the most sanitary practice. But then again, a lot of things in those days weren't. To this very day, when I'm making syrup for my hummingbird feeder, I test whether or not the sugar has gone into solution by rubbing the mixture between my fingers.

After the sugar had gone into solution, we then added the proper amount of concentrate. It always came in three or four different containers, and we would pour the contents of each into the tank with the appropriate coloring and flavoring. There was always a great temptation when the syrup was finally mixed to drink a bottle of the straight syrup. The strawberry flavor was a great favorite.

In later years, particularly in the years after World War Two, many labor saving devices began to appear on the scene. For example, the manual paddles that we used to mix the concentrate together gave way to electric motors that were put directly into the syrup tanks. These motors could mix the syrup into solution in about five minutes! Before, it had taken a great deal longer. Also, the first forklift and pallet truck that I ever saw appeared shortly after the war. The first pallet trucks and forklifts appeared in the early Fifties. We had one, and it was certainly a great innovation. We would stack the cases three by two, six cases per layer. Each pallet could be filled six layers high. They were crisscrossed halfway up a couple of times because they were tilted back on a forklift truck. It was quite a labor saving device to load a truck in such a short period of time.

As time went on, sanitation became an ever-increasing consideration. Coca-Cola plants in general were always kept very clean for a variety of reasons. First, there was the Food and Drug Administration. A group of local and state inspectors from the FDA would check periodically to make sure everything was kept clean and orderly.   In addition, Coca-Cola had its own team of inspectors who went around taking all sorts of exotic, bacterial tests and swabbings of our equipment. We ourselves were required to measure our syrup content and mail it in bottles every so often so that The Coca-Cola Company could perform tests on our carbonation and syrup. Later, they would send us back the lab reports. Over time these sanitation requirements became more and more demanding. However, we were all very understanding because we knew we were producing a product that people put into their mouths. We all felt very proud knowing that we ran a clean and sanitary plant.

Another important reason for keeping things clean—the machinery in particular—was that every drink we bottled was produced on the same line. If we made a run of one kind of drink, and then turned around to run a line of a different drink without cleaning the machines properly, then we would run the risk of having the second batch tasting a bit like the first. NuGrape, in particular, was notorious for leaving a lingering taste on a piece of equipment. To avoid mixing the flavors, we began to clean the line very meticulously between runs, even to the point of using chlorinated water and soda water rinse. The trouble then was that chlorine residue could give Coca-Cola the most terrible taste. I have a very sensitive taste for the presence of chlorine, so that even when I was very young I would be called back and asked, "Have we got all the chlorine out?" I could taste very minute quantities—probably one part in a million.

One of our co-owners, Dargan Cole, bought a system that used only electricity to treat the water. Dargan was the son of Mr. Ed Cole and managed the Cartersville plant. He claimed that by charging and discharging the water, all the microbes, iron, and algae could be killed. In reality, all that system did was use up electricity and money.

Yet another difficulty we faced in the production of Coca-Cola was the need to make the water from different cities taste as much alike as possible. The first water treatment system that we used was fairly simple. We would take the city water and introduce it into a huge tank. Next, we would increase the chlorine to a level much higher than that of the city system. We added to the mixture a chemical called ferrous sulfate, which turned the water brown and caused a precipitate called floc to form. After a period of about 12 to 14 hours, the precipitate would settle down to the bottom of the tank, pulling along with it any algae or bacteria that had been in the water. This precipitate was called floc. Finally, we would skim the water on the top and run it through huge activated charcoal filters. The charcoal filters removed any remaining chlorine from the water. Sand and gravel filters removed any remaining vestige of debris.

By the end of the procedure, we had the most sparkling clean, pure water that anyone could imagine. It was far better than the water from the city system. An interesting sideline is that when we would take people through the plant to show them how pure our water was, the ferrous sulfate and the iron in the coagulation process would be draining out the bottom of the tanks. It looked a bit like mud, but it was actually the ferrous sulfate precipitating out. We would tell people that what they were seeing was what we got out of the city water! We were a bit misleading... but many people were impressed, and we figured it might make people drink Coca-Cola before they would drink the city water. In truth, the water we used WAS far purer than the city water anyway.

I would like to include here some information about the rationing days of the 1940's. One product that was rationed terribly in those days was metal—metal of any kind. I can remember that we would go around collecting metal cans and then send them to crown manufacturers so that we could have lids for our bottles. Another thing we did was to go around to all the crown catchers. (Crown catchers were the little boxes on the coolers that caught the crowns after they were removed from the bottles.) I can remember sitting and prying the cork out of all the crowns so that they would be clean. We had a little machine that could press and reform them. Of course, we had to put in a new cork or a new rubber liner.

Another product that was rationed in those days was sugar. And because sugar was rationed, syrup was rationed as well. There was a formula for determining how much sugar we were allowed. I never knew exactly how this formula came about, but I suppose that the government looked at how much Coca-Cola we sold in 1940 and then rationed us that amount of sugar to use each year throughout the entire war. I'm not entirely sure why it was necessary to ration sugar; I suppose it had something to do with the cessation of merchant shipping from the Philippines, Cuba, and other places where sugar was grown. But for some reason, sugar was very tightly rationed.

The syrup rationing continued until 1947, but why it lasted that long, I do not know. I do remember very clearly the day it was announced that syrup would no longer be rationed. We bottled Coca-Cola's for three straight days day and night the second that the rationing ended. After that, we put on two shifts to keep up with demand. Royce Peugh, a production superintendent; Jim Lumpkin, who we called Razorback; and I would go down to the plant at 3:00 in the morning to fire up the boilers so that the soakers could get going. We would bottle on up to about 1:00 in the afternoon, after which another crew would come in and bottle until 8:00 or 9:00 in the evening. The demand for Coca-Colas was so great that a line that just ran 6 or 7 hours a day would just not keep up.

Convention, Advertising, and College

The first convention that I attended was the 1947 American Bottlers of Carbonated Beverages Convention. It was right after World War Two, and the first of the really good equipment was beginning to come on line. So we gathered up a bunch of folks and went to Atlantic City. Bud West, Henry Stone, Millard Fincher, and I all went along. The trip from Atlanta to Atlantic City on the train took about two days and one night. I was only sixteen years old, and for me, it was quite a trip.

I remember one or two interesting things about our trip. For example, I remember Bud West and I having our picture taken. The photographers made Bud and me sit on a horse and buggy, and Bud gave me a cigar to put in my mouth.

Me and Bud West Atlantic City 1947

Alfred, Bud West, Willie, Me, Clarence Archer, and Bill Brisendine

I also remember two of the speakers who spoke at the convention. One was a gentleman by the name of Harrison Jones, who was the vice president of the Coca-Cola Company and quite a delightful gentleman. His son, Gordon Jones, subsequently became president of Fulton National Bank, which was later sold to Bank South. Gordon and I later served for several years together as Atlanta Gas Light Board Members. Mr. Harrison Jones was a huge mountain of man, with gray wavy hair and big thick glasses. The thing I remember about Harrison was how profane he was. In private conversations, every other word was a curse word. But he was one of the most dynamic speakers and dynamic men that has ever lived—very much hell fire and damnation, almost like a preacher.

The other gentleman that I remember quite well was Deloney Sledge. Deloney was a little bitty sort of a pipsqueak—a little bald headed fellow who looked to me like a banty rooster. He was extremely humorous, and his forte was advertising. He was the advertising manager for Coca-Cola, as I recall, and he would give very perceptive talks about what motivated people and how to do advertising. Some of his slogans that I remember were "Around the corner from everywhere" and "Thirst knows no season."

Very soon after my first convention, the 12 ounce bottle came along. Of course, in those days the bottle was made available only by our competition. The only size bottle that we handled was the 6 ½ ounce returnable. It wasn't until much later that the 10 ounce, the 32, and many other sizes came along.

While we're on the subject of advertising, perhaps I should comment on some of the early Coca-Cola advertisers that I remember. The head of the Rome Advertising Department in the early, early days was a fellow named Robert Redden. Robert was a very tall, spare man—a very gentle giant, and quite a talented artist. He created pen and ink sketches on his own for many years as a hobby and eventually became quite famous as a local artist. Robert left the company somewhere in the late 1950's to become an independent artist. He subsequently made drawings

This is a Robert Redden drawing of the Cedartown Coca-Cola Plant. This plant was built in the late 70s when they moved from Main Street

of all the Coca-Cola plants. The originals are now in

Robert Redden's version of the Fort Valley Coca-Cola Plant

the possession of Al and Mike.

    Robert's drawings, particularly the originals of some of his pen and inks, are now extremely famous. I have in my possession two or three original drawings that he had made into Christmas cards and sent to me. Sometime in the early 1980's, I found out that the Berry College Journalism Department was producing a series of video documentaries, and I asked them to create a 30-minute documentary of Robert's life. I have got a copy of it, and I'm sure Berry does as well.

    In the early days, the paint shop was located on North Broad, behind what is now Jennings Funeral Home. My grandfather had originally bought the building as a precaution, in case we someday outgrew the plant on 5th Avenue. However, sometime in the early 1930's or perhaps the late 1920's, he decided to use the North Broad building for other purposes. The front part was sold to the Jennings Brothers, Frank and Jim, to form what is Jennings Funeral Home. My grandfather kept or leased (I never did know which) a big barn in back of the lot. That was where he placed the sign department. Robert Redden presided over the venture together with Henry Stone.

Henry was quite a character—a fellow who was always getting into some sort of a scrape. He took a liking to alcohol— not so much that people today would call him an alcoholic, but he certainly did like to go drink when he got away from his wife, Grace. Grace was one of the loveliest ladies I've ever known. Henry was a great fellow to go on a convention with because he was so much fun. He would tell jokes and would always be so full of laughter. He was a wonderful human being. He also happened to be a very talented sign painter. Once or twice a year, Henry and Robert and later on, Harold Frazier would go off to Cedartown, Fort Valley, or various other places for two or three days to paint walls and signs.

Harold Frazier, who inherited the mantle of the advertising department, was another wonderful human being. He was probably one of the most Christian, charitable people I've ever known in my life. Harold and I had a very close relationship that still exists to this day. He is even kind enough to do little odd jobs for me. I treasure having Harold and his wife Edith as friends.

During the 1950's Dalton had its own sign painting department. A fellow named Oscar Rollins was in charge of the department. He was another one of those sign painters who enjoyed a good time and who tended to overindulge in alcohol. It seems that the sign painting business attracted this sort of person. (Harold Frazier was a notable exception. As far as I know, he never took the first drink of anything alcoholic in all of his life.)

During the summers of 1948 through 1952, I worked at the Coca-Cola plant. Many of

The memories I've described about mixing syrup and that sort of thing took place in those days. I graduated from Darlington High School in 1948 and went to college at Washington & Lee. The record probably shows that I was only 16 ½ when I entered college, which was very young. I was, of course, terribly immature and not terribly big. I think I weighed about 128 pounds soaking wet.

Frank-16 years old

In 1951, while I was a junior and senior in college, North Korea invaded South Korea. The situation created what turned out to be some rather dramatic changes at home and abroad. My father had predicted in 1948 that there would be another war soon and that the best thing for me to do would be to get an education. So I proceeded to go to college. I graduated from Washington & Lee in June of 1952 at age 20. I was fortunate enough to secure an appointment to Navy OCS, and I reported there in September of 1952 to obtain my commission. I received my commission on December 21, 1952 when I was ten days short of being 21 years old.

So there I was, brand new to the Navy, ready to go to war, and not quite 21. I did end up going to Korea, spending three years in the Navy, and then coming back. But that's the subject of another chapter. While I was in the navy, my Uncle William (Bill) G. Brisendine passed away. He had been the owner of the Fort Valley Coca-Cola Bottling Company, and he and his wife, Will Sharp (my Grandmother Barron's half-sister), had no children. Therefore, the Fort Valley Coca-Cola Plant was passed to the Barron family. I'm not entirely certain of the specifics of how Uncle Bill originally acquired the plant, but I've been told that my grandfather loaned Bill about $1200 in the early 1910's. Bill then bought the franchise for Fort Valley Coca-Cola and ran it very successfully until his death in 1952. Bill was quite a golfer and was very well respected in the community. When my father and my uncle went to Fort Valley to take over the plant, they found everything in very good condition.

Mississippi Clark was the manager of the Fort Valley plant. He had worked closely with Uncle Bill, but he became somewhat of a weight around Alfred's shoulders. I think Alfred eventually ran him off. Mississippi was quite a character, though, and his great asset was his incredible skill in the game of golf. Before Uncle Bill passed away, he and Mississippi would go play golf every Wednesday and Saturday. They rather let the plant go to itself, which was not uncommon in those days. In the 1930's, 1940's, and 1950's, it was rather well conceded that all a person had to do to run a good Coca-Cola plant was to get the trucks out, collect the money, and attend a convention every now and then. Before Pepsi Cola became a strong contender, the Coca-Cola business was to a great degree nothing but a cash cow.

The Coosa Queen, Engagement to Anne, Dalton

In December of 1955, after my time in the Navy, I was ready to tackle the world of Coca-Cola. First, I went to Florida with my mother for about three or four weeks to become readjusted to civilian life. Then, on February 12, 1956, I went to work.

There's a somewhat interesting story about how I remember the specific date of February 12. While I was spending about six weeks at home, some good friends of mine found out about an old flat bottomed, two vehicle ferry that had been put up for sale. They were Penn Nixon, Martin Bradshaw, and Hines Daniel. Later on, Porter Grant bought into the deal as well. He was a great addition and a great friend. The boat was owned by D. O. Johnson, a fellow who had run the ferryboat roughly between Turkey Mountain and Armuchee before the Georgia 140 Bridge was built. The four of us each put up $25 so we could pay the $100 D. O. charged for his old ferry. On February 11, which was a Sunday, we all went up the river to D.O. Johnson's place to pick up the boat. (I took along Anne West, who later became my wife. She and I had been dating since Christmas.) We arrived at D.O.'s around 9:00 that morning. With the help of Penn's 14 foot, 20 horsepower runabout and a number of lines carefully assembled to secure the ferryboat, down the river we came. Anne's mother thought we were absolutely insane (and she probably was correct). The project took us all day. Once we finally got to Rome at about 3:00 in the afternoon, we took the boat down to the Coosa Country Club and tied it up.

That entire spring, we spent every Saturday and Sunday afternoon working on the ferryboat to convert it into a houseboat. We mounted a board across the back and attached three outboard motors, the center of which was attached to a large wagon wheel that was used for steering. Our boat became known to us as the "Coosa Queen". We had some wonderful beer parties and cookouts on that old boat. Needless to say, people would often stop and look at us as we would go up and down the rivers because the boat was a rather outlandish sight. The three rivers were, of course the Coosa, the Oostanaula and the Etowah. Our Sunday afternoon excursions became somewhat famous in the area.

The following fall, when the winter rains came and the dry spells came in right behind them, tying the ferryboat up to the dock at the Coosa Country Club became quite a problem. (Incidentally, the reason the Coosa Country Club was so willing to let us tie the boat up to their riverbank was because we were among their greatest consumers of beer.) The rise and fall of the river during those days would tend to tilt the ferryboat, and we couldn't keep it pushed away from the bank. When it tilted down, the boat would fill up with water—so much that on one or two occasions we had to attach five Coca-Cola trucks and a pulley to the ferry so we could pull it out of the river. After about the second time that this happened, however, we decided that the ferry was becoming more than we could handle, so we sold it to a fireman by the name of Sid Johnson. Sid floated it down the river on high water one time and converted it into a permanent house at Lake Weiss. As far as I know, that's where the boat remains today.

As I mentioned before, during Christmas that year I began dating Anne West. She was a schoolteacher, born and raised near Shannon. I remembered seeing her around as a child because our parents had been great friends. However, I didn't know her well until I was older. How Anne and I came to be engaged is another great story.

I was travelling a great deal in those days, going to Dalton, Carrollton, and other places to stay for a week or so at a time. I was primarily learning the territory and learning the people.

Occasionally, I would go to a Rotary Club luncheon as a guest of one of the managers. But mostly I spent my days riding trucks—"riding the routes" as we called it. I considered myself enormously popular. Every day, the salespeople would go by to see whom the manager had assigned me to ride with that day. I assumed that because I was the boss's son and because I thought myself extremely likeable, I was the preferred companion of all the salesmen. Of course, the real reason behind their preference didn't occur to me for a while. Each truck had a salesman and a helper on it, and the helper's work was cut by about fifty percent if I happened to be along for the ride. I was terribly eager to prove what a hard worker I was, so I worked harder than anyone else. It wasn't my popularity that kept them asking if it was their turn to have me along on the truck. It was my extra pair of hands, strong back, and weak mind.

On one of my week long trips in the spring of 1957, I was working at the Dalton Coca-Cola plant. I took my suppers at the Dalton Hotel and spent the night there as well. The hotel had no air conditioning; consequently, at night I had to keep the windows open. The train came by every 45 minutes and woke me up. It was always very hot. One night, I thought to myself, "There's not but one way I'm going to get out of this situation, and that's to get married."

The next day, I went to the Coca-Cola plant and asked to speak to the manager, Clarence Archer. I told him, "I gotta go to Rome, and I gotta go now." Anne was teaching school at Model Elementary—4th grade. I called her out of class and proposed to her right then and there. I was wearing my Coca-Cola uniform and everything, which may be a first. We were married on June 21. I loved her dearly, as I do now. Sometimes, I jokingly tell her that if the Dalton

Hotel would have had air conditioning, I might not be a married man today!

DALTON

I never did know how our family got involved in Dalton. I do know that it was around 1920 or 1921. I suspect it was owned by Chattanooga and they decided to sell it to my Grandfather and the Sapp family.

There are many interesting things to tell about Dalton. Dalton, in those days, was a town of spread houses and chenille plants. Perhaps the chenille industry is a topic that requires a bit of explanation.

The chenille industry all started when Mrs. Whitener developed the skill to make bedspreads. Not long afterwards, the old U.S. Highway 41 became known as "bedspread alley" because of all the chenille bedspreads and bathrobes that were displayed for sale alongside the road. When we would ride up and down Highway 41 and see all the chenille crafts with their elaborate designs, we would laugh and say that if a person didn't have a bathrobe with a peacock on it, that person just wasn't "in."

An explanation of how chenille was made might be of interest. To make chenille, a piece of yarn was pulled through a backing usually made of canvas. The strings of the yarn were left sticking out. These strings could either be looped or cut. The simple technique of weaving was mechanically handled by placing six needles side by side so that a row of tufts, or "loops," could be made. This development sped up the industry greatly. I can recall riding the routes in my early days in Dalton, seeing spread houses that were literally full of women, young and old, sitting there with yarn machines and bathrobes and bedspreads and all manner of throw rugs.

What really put the carpet industry on its feet was when technology got to the point that a person could tuft carpet in very tight, six feet wide sections. As soon there began to be machine woven carpet, sometimes made of wool but mostly made of nylon and other synthetics. The industry just mushroomed at first, but then it died down. That's where Shaw Industry basically got its start. Bob Shaw (a contemporary of mine) and his father ran an operation called Star Dye. There's a long story about Shaw Industry and how it got started from dying carpets, but that's been addressed by Shaw Industry historians. As the industry grew and carpets came to be tufted in sections twelve feet wide, it got to be a very labor intensive business. This and many other technological improvements changed the tenor of the town of Dalton dramatically.

I would often go to Dalton, Carrollton, or other places for the day. If I had a particular route that I wanted to ride, or there was some particular thing that I wanted to do, I would just get up at 5:00 in the morning, get in my car, and drive up there. There was a time in those days when I was putting anywhere from 45,000 to 55,000 miles a year on my car. That lasted up until we bought an airplane in connection with the Valdosta plant.

The old Dalton Coca-Cola plant, a very small sort of bottling operation, was located downtown across

This is the Robert Redden version of the Dalton Coca-Cola plant as it looked when first constructed in 1954

from the Oakwood Café. Ray Jones was one of the top salesmen of the Dalton plant—that I do remember. Also there was a fellow by the name of Ledford, and some other folks whose names escape me now. But in about 1953 or 1954, Daddy, Alfred, and Clarence decided the thing to do was to build a new plant in Dalton, and so they did out on South Thornton Avenue.

There was a wonderful gentleman named Clarence Archer who came to be the manager of the Dalton Coca-Cola plant. Clarence came to work at Coca-Cola in about 1925 as a route salesman. I can still remember him telling me stories about those early days in Dalton. He said then that there were only about four routes. The bottling was handled by a crew of perhaps two or three men because the machine was very small. The trucks would come in; the crews would take off the empty bottles and restock the truck with full ones, and then off the trucks would go once again. In 1927, when my grandfather and my father had the opportunity to buy about 2/3 of Dalton Coca-Cola, they gave Clarence the opportunity to buy a portion of it as well. So Clarence locked up his truck and went with my granddaddy down to the bank. My granddaddy borrowed the money for Clarence to buy twelve percent—a share worth about $3500—and within an hour Clarence was back to finishing his route. He used to marvel about how easily the transaction was done and how impossible it would be for something like that to happen today.

Clarence Archer soon became the manager of Dalton Coca-Cola, which he remained for many, many years until his retirement around 1978. He was one of the charter members of the Dalton Rotary Club. (This indicates something of the significance of the status of Coca-Cola managers in the mid 1930's.) Clarence was probably one of the best known men in Dalton. He was certainly regarded as a leader of his church and a leader of his community. He died in December of 1999 at the age of 91.

There was a third, very minor, stockholder group in the Dalton Coca-Cola plant, and that was the Sapp family. The principal stockholders were Richard and Julian Sapp, along with their sister. Julian was the one with whom I dealt. He was a very fine gentleman and a lawyer by trade. In the early days, we had tried to buy the Sapp interests, which had amounted to around nine percent of the whole. Unfortunately, they never would sell. As Julian told me, his father on his death bed had told Julian never to sell the Coca-Cola stock. As it turned out, this was probably a wise decision. At the final sale in 1985, their share amounted to several millions of dollars.

One of the main issues in the soft drink business during these years was the placing of automatic coin vending machines. This was a very profitable business and one which occupied a great deal of our time and a huge amount of our capital investment. A vending machine of the day would run anywhere from $250 to $500-$600 depending on how large and complex they were and whether they would handle one or more flavors. There were several manufacturers and we bought coolers generally in tractor trailer lots for which you received a discount. The competitive side of this question was the fact that if you had a Coca-Cola machine in an exclusive account, for example a service station, and your competitor (Pepsi Cola) were able to place a machine beside yours, it would not cut your sales half into but it would certainly take a certain percentage away. For that reason it was our object to have what we called exclusive accounts. We desired to have all of our accounts to become exclusive accounts, that is, they sold only our products. This of course as the years went on included Coca-Colas in more than one size, Grape, Orange, Sprite or some other flavors so we were able to sell or supply an entire line of flavors. One of the tactics we used whenever a competitive cooler was placed was to attempt to get rid of it. In Dalton, our main tactic was to offer a bonus or bounty as it were, to the salesman who got rid of a competitive machine on his route. I kept a list of every single competitive cooler in both Cartersville and Dalton for many, many years. Once a week I would go over with the manager of the plant this list to see if we were making any progress with cleaning up the territory. Dalton at one time had less than 25 competitive vending machines in the entire territory. This compared with our 750 or 800 coolers so we completely dominated as you can tell. I had a $100 cash bonus payable to any salesman who reported that he had gotten rid of a particular competitive machine. One Monday morning I came in and was greeted by the Sales Manager with the great news that they had gotten rid of 4 of the 20 some odd coolers over the weekend. I said what a wonderful story! I would love to know how you did this so I could take this tactic to some other plants and perhaps we can get rid of some other coolers in other territories. He kept hemming and hawing and finally I said "Look. How did you do it?" He looked at me straight in the eye and said "Mr. B you don't want to know." I knew that something very wicked was going on. I discontinued the bounty soon thereafter because I figured we were probably doing something illegal.

Carrollton and Competition

Other than Dalton (and, of course, Rome), the other place where I spent a great deal of time in my earlier career was in Carrollton. Simpson Carter was a particular gentleman from Carrollton who stands out in my memory. His sister, Sarah Keown, worked in the courthouse over across the street in Rome. Simpson was a great Christian sort of fellow, and we would often go to conventions together down in Savannah. We would stay at the old Oglethorpe Hotel on the Intra-Coastal Waterway. There were always big cocktail parties for all of the Georgia Soft Drink Association members—Bud West, Alfred, Daddy, Jane, and Mama would usually go along as well. The ladies would go off and do their thing, and the gentlemen would go to the meetings. At these cocktail parties, Simpson's wife would enjoy a little sip every now and then, to Simpson's great displeasure. I remember one time when I, the polite young man, asked Mrs. Carter if she would care for something to drink. Simpson replied, "She'll have a Coca-Cola." I can't remember whether I did this intentionally or whether I even knew about it beforehand, but I do remember that she ended up with a Coca-Cola that had a little bourbon in it, and that suited her just fine. When I came back about thirty minutes later and asked, "Mrs. Carter, can I get you another Coca-Cola?", her answer was "Yes, just like that last one!" Simpson never knew!

In about 1959, Simpson decided to forego his position as manager of the Carrollton plant and run for tax commissioner. There was a young route supervisor named Bill Hooper, a supervisor down in Cedartown, whom Alfred wanted to take Simpson's place. Bill was an aggressive young man, a red-headed fellow who was stout as a bull. He was just a wonderful person. But Bill Hooper did not know Carrollton. For some reason, Alfred decided that the existing route manager was not good enough to show Bill the ropes. Because I had spent so much time in Carrollton, he gave the task to me. Bill and I went down to Carrollton, and for two weeks we would just ride from one end of that territory to the other. I knew where the boundaries were, having ridden through that area for years. We would stop and chat with folks, even though I might not know them, to look at their displays and take notes. Then would we ride around a little more and meet the route salesmen. We

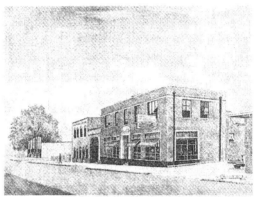

Robert Redden's version of the Carrollton Coca-Cola plant as it looked in the mid 60s.

would talk to them and see how things were going.

I can remember that I when I was driving to Carrollton, I would get up at 5:00 a.m. and take about an hour to drive there. That early in the morning, there weren't that many people out on the roads and there weren't many state patrolmen, for which I was eternally grateful. We never did worry too much about the state patrol because we had a long standing custom of giving a Christmas turkey or ham to every patrolman in Cartersville, Cedartown, Summerville, and Carrollton. (There wasn't a station in Rome.) In those days, the state patrol was very politically oriented. They all knew us and we all knew them—all the sergeants and even the North Georgia captain. The idea of being arrested was a bit removed from my mind because we knew them all anyway and we had given them all a turkey. If I did go too fast and was pulled over, the patrolman would simply say, "Frank, keep it slow, somebody might see you. You have just got to behave yourself."

As I said, I would leave Rome at 5:00 to go to Carrollton and arrive at about 6:00 in the morning. Sometimes I would beat Bill Hooper getting there. We would go up and meet with the salesmen, and then I would ride a different route or I would spend time with Bill. Around 5:30 or so in the evening, when all the money was in and all the trucks were locked up, I would get in my car and drive home. Sometimes I would get back as late as 7:00. The difficulty in this was that I never saw Frank III, a baby then, except for on Saturdays and Sundays. Even in those days, we were working at least a half day, sometimes even 3/4 of a day, on Saturday. I was home most Saturdays by noon. Alfred had finally convinced my dad that we didn't have to work six full days a week and that in fact, the salespeople weren't going to work six full days a week. America was becoming too modernized for that. A great many things were being written about how to treat employees and how to be a modern manager. Among these things was the idea that employees wouldn't work sixty hours a week. Therefore, we began phasing back.

One of the other phenomena that was beginning to occur in those days was the phenomenon of competition. As I stated earlier, back in the 1940's and early 1950's the six and a half ounce bottle was the only one on the market. Then there began to be some larger products, such as Double Cola and Royal Crown, which were ten and twelve ounce products. Pepsi Cola soon developed a very famous slogan that said, "Pepsi Cola hits the spot. Twelve full ounces, that's a lot! Twice as much for a nickel, too. Pepsi Cola's the drink for you." I remember that very well, and we all laughed at it. Pepsi-Cola became known to us as "belly wash." People of that day were interested in quality, or so we thought, and so they were until economics began to be a real factor. The twelve ounce size was needed for a growing family, and wives could buy twelve ounces of Pepsi for the same price as they could buy six and half ounces of Coca-Cola. It's not hard to guess which one they started buying. The kids didn't really know the difference, anyway.

Competition became a fact of life for us. I suppose it was to our credit, or to the credit of the organization, that we saw the impact of this competition perhaps a bit earlier than some of the other Coca-Cola bottlers. The Coca-Cola Company soon announced a trial period of its ten ounce product. Alfred and Daddy had a fit to go down to Atlanta and get them because they saw what was happening to our business. As a side note, it's rather interesting today to note that our major competition, as we perceived it in those days, was not Pepsi Cola, but rather Double Cola. Double Cola was a small locally owned company out of Chattanooga. It was a good product with a good taste to it, and evidently it was right cheap to produce because Double Cola had been able to cut their prices tremendously. We had many arguments through the years about price cutting and how we thought the competition was able to do it. That was a long standing battle.

In 1959 or 1960, we convinced the Coca-Cola Company to let us be a test market for the larger sized bottle. Because all of our equipment was outfitted for a six and a half ounce bottle, the need to run a bottle that was an inch or two taller was a major obstacle. There were people around who decided that they knew how to make the necessary modifications. They would take the washers, cut them in two, and stretch them out. This made it possible for the 10 ounce products to be run through the old six and half ounce bottle washers. But to do so was a major commitment. Everything had to be changed. We changed the filling height, put about 1.54 ounces of syrup in the ten ounce bottles (as compared to one ounce in the six and half ounce bottles), changed the syrup cups, and changed the mixers over. We decided to perform the changeover because we saw that we would have to match the competitor, price for price and ounce for ounce. It was not an easy decision.

Even more difficulties arose when it came to distributing these 10 ounce bottles. We had to face such dilemmas, for example, as how to sell the larger sized bottles through our existing vending machines. Some of the old vending machines could be modified to sell the ten ounce package, but the vast majority of them couldn't. Thus was developed the first vending machine able to sell the ten ounce bottles.

Another great consideration was pricing the new product. It was our feeling that since we were giving customers .54 more ounces, we should perhaps charge them 54 percent more. But the problem was more complicated than that. No one knew exactly how much more it cost to produce the new product. The additional water needed cost virtually nothing, but the time of bottling was extended because the new bottles took a bit longer to fill. Delivery costs were somewhat higher because not as many bottles would fit on the trucks. It was very difficult to determine exactly what all of these incremental cost increases would amount to. In order to create a compromise, we ended up charging 80 cents a case for the 6 ½ ounce products and one dollar for the ten ounce.

For dealers, the addition of the new sized product was a much simpler situation. If a store manager sold his Coca-Colas in an open top cooler (as he did more often than not), it was just as easy for him to stock the cooler with 10 ounce bottles as it had been to stock the 6 ½ ounce ones. But when a customer would come in, put down a nickel, and ask for a Coca-Cola, the manager now had to decide whether the man would get the ten ounce size or the 6 ½ ounce. Usually, the dealer would simply increase the price on all of his Coca-Cola products, and this became the standard price.

    In this pricing discussion, for us there were some huge emotional arguments. My dad just didn't want to leave the nickel price. He said that we would ruin ourselves and that he just wouldn't agree to us raising the price. Of course, we didn't want to raise the price either. But this was in the 1960's, and inflationary pressures were beginning to occur everywhere. All of our employees needed raises. The price of bottles was increasing. In general, our expenses were climbing. We just couldn't live with a price for the regular 6 ½ ounce Coca-Cola, a price that was established 1930's. This price was 80 cents a case. Later on when the ten ounce was first introduced it came out at 96 cents. Why we picked that price, I don't know. The first price increase was to keep the 80 cent price and to sell king size for a dollar. Later on we went to a dollar for the regular and a dollar twenty for the king size.

The 1950s and '60s

Some of my most prominent memories from the late 1950's and early 1960's involve riding the Pocket, riding the Loop, and going to Calhoun. I still rode routes a good bit in those days although, to my disappointment, my route riding days would soon come to an end.

Riding a route was an interesting thing to do. In particular, I used to like to ride what we called "The Pocket Route," serviced in those days by a fellow named E.K. Pope. It didn't carry a very large volume of business, but it was a very tiring sort of route for several reasons. First of all, the roads were all dirt roads. They went up towards Summerville, then towards Armuchee and Everett Springs, and finally over to Floyd Springs and Lake Marvin. When I would drive it in the summertime, I had to leave my windows down on account of the heat. I almost suffocated from the dust in the road. Coca-Cola trucks, at best, weren't the fastest animal on the road, so everyone would be trying to get around me and in front of me. I would be eating dust all day long.

Perhaps it would be interesting and informative to describe a typical sales call that might be made by a Coca-Cola truck in the 60's, 70's and 80's and earlier even. It would be one thing to describe a call on a large supermarket such as a Piggly Wiggly, Colonial or Big Apple as were common in those days. It would be another thing to describe a sales call on an industrial account such as West Point Pepperell. In addition to those types of accounts there would be the myriads of Doctors' offices, jewelry stores, beauty parlors, etc. which were a large part of our system. The call I'm going to describe would be what we would refer to as a 'Mom and Pop' grocery store because we were very dependent upon them. While the volume wasn't as great, the total volume of these types of outlets added up to a large portion of our sales.

Upon approaching a typical 'Mom and Pop' grocery store, the first thing that the salesman would do would be to observe, according to the protocol or "planned call" as we called it, the outside signs. If they needed repainting or if the lettering was bad. It was our philosophy to have as many signs on stores and buildings including walls, hangouts, window posters, etc., as we could. If this was all okay he would then go inside and observe whatever inside signs there were such as, if there were a soda fountain there would be signs advertising ice cold Coca-Cola for a nickel or ten cents or whatever. There would be signs designating an area where the cartons and the case goods would be displayed. There would be an arrow sometimes indicating where the vending machines or the cooler would be located. After assuring himself that all the signs were okay he would then look to see what shape the stock was in. This would involve looking at the display stock and then perhaps a trip to the back room where extra stock would be stored in inventory for filling up the racks or displays as required. He would then go to wherever the empty bottles would be stored which had accumulated since his last call. He and his helper would arrange these bottles in some order so they could be counted and the quantity of empty bottles determined.

Now came the question of whether the man was a delivery man or a salesman. If he were a true salesman he would say in order to fill the inventory up to where it was on my last call two days ago it would take X number of cases. However, if I can talk the store owner into increasing his display of cartons at the end of an aisle perhaps I can increase the display space which would virtually automatically lead to increased sales. This was a question whether he could persuade the gentleman or lady in question to invest in additional inventory and this of course is where salesmanship came in.

Once he had determined the quantity to be delivered then he and the helper would go to the truck. They would then bring the required amounts of the Coca-Colas in whatever size and or flavor required to fill the displays up and fill up the inventory. When this was compared back against the empty bottle inventory as a plus or minus, he would then present the store manager or owner with a bill. He could be paid either by check, charge account or in cash. This would be the end of the transaction whereupon he would go to the next store.

As the years went on particularly early after WWII the process of a 'planned call' became more codified and put into more formal structure. There was a professional company by the name of Jam Handy Company who had representatives in Atlanta. These people would occasionally put on training sessions for not only all of our sales managers but the salesmen as well. They would travel around to the plants and you would have, for example a dinner and then perhaps a one and half hour meeting after dinner where the Jam Handy people would have play role acting and work out a planned call. Since this was not too long after WWII these were all very new and somewhat modernistic ideas in everyone's minds. But, once you have heard the planned sales call that I have just outlined it was all very logical and very well done. This was used by the Coca-Cola soft drink industry worldwide and was very successful.

A gourmet meal on a country route was what we used to refer to as "the sardine and soda crackers luncheon." That was when we would go into a store at about noon or 1:00, starving to death, and buy a pack of soda crackers, some sardines, and a Coca-Cola—to be eaten on a bank or the edge of the road somewhere. It was the best we could hope for because there weren't any restaurants or anything of that nature up in those routes. But they were a lot of fun.

Of course, riding the other routes was also a lot of fun. I always particularly enjoyed going to Calhoun. I also really enjoyed working Broad Street in Rome because everyone knew everybody and that made it a very lively sort of place. I would go to Wyatt's, Fahy's, Huffman-Salmon's, and into the basements of all these buildings. I would go in the back of Esserman's and into all the dentist's and doctor's offices up on the third floor of the old First National Bank building, poking around in the storage buildings of all these places. GE, or General Electric, came to town in 1952 or 1953 while I was in the service. It was always a lot of fun to go there and watch them make transformers.

Other great places to go were Eton and Chatsworth, little mill towns up towards Dalton. I remember a fellow by the name of Robert Maples who worked the Chatsworth and Murray County route. In those days, Murray County had to stretch to deserve a full route. I seem to remember that Robert worked Chatsworth and Murray County three days a week and worked another route the rest of the week. Of course, my memory could be wrong.

Somewhere about this time, two more drinks came along: Fanta, which was primarily an orange drink, and Bubble Up, which was a good product that sold well. Then, the Coca-Cola Company came out with a new product called Sprite. Sprite, with its little picture of a pixie fellow behind the crown, was very attractive and very lovable. Most of us picked up Sprite fairly quickly and dropped Bubble Up. There were other bottlers in those days, however, who sold Seven Up. The Coca-Cola Bottling Company in Huntsville, Alabama is still quite a large producer of Seven Up. In fact, I think they bottle for most of the state of Alabama.

The ABCB, or American Bottlers of Carbonated Beverages, changed their name to the National Soft Drink Association, or NSDA, sometime in the 1950's. We went to many conventions in those days, in such places as Chicago, Atlantic City, Dallas, San Francisco, Los Angeles, Detroit and Cleveland. During the 1950's, the big NSDA exhibitions took place every other year because the conventions included demonstrations of full bottling operations. On the off years, the association would hold a much smaller exhibition, which consisted mainly of meetings, seminars on sanitation and advertising, and such well-known keynote speakers as the president of Pepsi or Coca-Cola.

Of course, there were always quite a few cocktail parties at these conventions. We would be assigned to go to a particular ballroom or meeting area where we would visit with the various bottlers. I remember that the Riverside Manufacturing Company, which made uniforms, always had a hospitality room. It was always a particular favorite with me. My mother and I used to love to go there because they had a fellow who could play the accordion. He would play songs that people would stand around in groups and sing. Mother and I both used to love to do that. There was also a fellow from the Pepsi Cola Company, a little bald headed man with a mustache, but I don't remember his name. He was one of the Pepsi Cola Company's top officers, and he would just arrange to meet there and sing with us. Then we would go down to the Liquid Carbonic Room or the Olin Matheson Chemical Company Room, eating and drinking and staying up until two or three o'clock at night. We always had such a great time.

Another interesting thing about the NSDA conventions was that each year, a different manufacturer of bottles would design a special souvenir bottle. They were all very colorful, with the date and the name of the convention site on them. If, for example, the convention was held in San Francisco, there would be a bottle with a little emblem of the San Francisco 49ers and a picture of Alcatraz. Or if we were in Atlantic City, the bottle would have a picture of the boardwalk. It soon became quite the thing to do to collect these bottles. I have a huge collection. I don't think I'm missing but perhaps two of the bottles.

The Coca-Cola Company would have their own conventions, separate from the NSDA meetings. They would have either one big, once a year meeting or several regional meetings. We would go and see the advertising plans for the year, including the new radio commercials, which were very popular in those days. The way to hear the radio ads was to buy a little record with the commercial on it. In the early days, there were 78 RPMs, but as time went on, we could buy smaller, 45 RPM records, which were about twice the size of a CD. There would be several different spots on the records, and you could choose the ones you liked and take them around to the local radio stations. Of course in later years, television became the big advertising medium. That's a story that I won't get into now.

Some of the interesting people that I remember from the 1950's and 1960's, all of whom were certainly older than me, were contemporaries of my father. The Coca-Cola Industry went through a series of less than stellar presidents in those days—Burt Nicholson and one or two others—who were not good for our business. Towards the end of the 1960's, as I recall, Lee Tally came along. He had been with the business a long time. He was a friend of the bottlers and a great individual. At the same time, there was Luke Smith. He became President of Coca-Cola USA under Lee Tally. Luke and his wife Claire were extremely close friends of the Barron family. I still see Claire, as she is a very loyal alumna of Shorter College. Luke always got along with the bottlers exceptionally well. He and Jim Wimberly, who had been involved with bottler relations in the Southeast for a number of years, were the two people who really kept the bottlers' best interests at heart.

From as far back as I can remember we were great users of White trucks. There was a reason for this. Mr. Ernest Woodruff, who had bought the Coca-Cola Company from Mr. Candler, had a son named Robert W. Woodruff, who was the head salesman for White

Motor Company. Naturally, many bottlers of Coca-Cola knew Robert Woodruff and were inclined to buy trucks from him. Josh Redmond, who worked the Piedmont, Alabama route, would drive no other truck than a White.

Mr. Woodruff was still in his prime in those days. He was in his seventies, I suppose, but he was still very much calling the shots. There are many stories about Mr. Woodruff in Atlanta. One specific anecdote about Mr. Woodruff that has been recounted by others better than me had to do with the funeral of Martin Luther King, Jr. When Reverend King was assassinated, there were fears of rioting and great chaos throughout the city of Atlanta. Mr. Woodruff called the mayor of Atlanta, whom I believe was Ivan Allen, and said he should hire the police and take whatever other precautions were necessary, all at Mr. Woodruff's expense. It was that simple. It would be unusual to hear of such an occurrence in modern times, but that was the way things were done in those days.

The 1960's were a decade of great change, both for the nation and for Coca-Cola. We broke the nickel price, brought in the ten ounce package, and began to think about the purchase of new bottling equipment. We were beginning to come into the Twentieth Century.

Charley Adams was an exceptional individual who probably understood the competitive stresses that were facing us in the 1960's more clearly than anyone. I never will forget a particular meeting I attended in North Carolina, at which Charley was warning us about the advent of Pepsi. In the middle of his speech, Charley reached over to the V83 vending machine standing next to him. All of a sudden, he popped a canvas from atop the machine and rolled it down. Painted on the front was a big blue machine that read "Pepsi Cola" for everyone to see. Charley said that we couldn't let Pepsi sneak up on us and take over our market so quickly. He cited some incidents from up in

North Carolina in which Pepsi salesmen would walk right into stores and better the vending deal. Sometimes they would even paint our Coca-Cola vending machines blue and stock Pepsi in them. The Pepsi salesmen converted numerous manufacturing plants from Coca-Cola to Pepsi Cola virtually overnight. In fact, at that time Pepsi Cola was actually outselling Coca-Cola in South Carolina. It was a frightening thing to those of us who didn't think that such a thing could ever happen. Charley Adams was a person who encouraged us to fight.

A major departure from our normal operation occurred in 1965, when Alfred, Daddy, and I decided that we wanted to expand. (Alfred's two sons, Al and Mike, were still in college in those days.) We knew that the only way to make our business grow was to buy some Coca-Cola plants, and we thought this sounded like a good idea. So when we found out that Valdosta Coca-Cola was for sale, we entered into some preliminary discussion. Mike, Al, Virginia, and I ended up buying Valdosta's Coca-Cola plant for $1,010,000—a price that we thought was more money than a fellow could ever see or pay back. But, considering what happened some twenty years later, that seemed a pittance.

We used the law firm of Sutherland, Asbell, and Brennen at that time—specifically, Mike Egan. Randolph Thrower, who subsequently became the head of the IRS, was Mike's mentor. He advised us as well. Cartersville and Dalton, my two operations, weren't requiring too much time, so Al, Daddy, and I decided that Valdosta would be on my hands. (Mike and Al were not there at this time, and of course Virginia had no interest in doing it.) We took Bill Evans, who was a supervisor in Rome, and made him manager of Valdosta. It was a great step forward for Bill. Tragically, Bill died of cancer in 1980. His wife, Carolyn, stayed in Valdosta after his death and has just recently passed away.

Cedartown

Cedartown was an operation where I spent a significant amount of time in the 1960's. It was only eighteen miles from plant to plant, so it was not a problem for me to get up at my regular time and arrive there at an early hour. I would arrive perhaps ten minutes after the manager did. A fellow by the name of P. A. Bond ran that plant for years and years. He was the manager all during World War II and until the late 1960's when he was offered a job at Atlanta Coca-Cola.

Cedartown was one of my favorite places. The city was in essence comprised of two smaller towns: the town of Cedartown itself and Rockmart. Rockmart is a small town over in East Polk County. The cement factory and perhaps one or two other places of importance were located there. The Goodyear Mills and Rome Plow were located in Cedartown proper. To me, Cedartown was such a great place because it was small—smaller than Carrollton and much smaller than Rome. It was the smallest plant we owned, with the exception of Fort Valley. For some reason, I never visited Fort Valley that much.

I remember some interesting characters from Cedartown. Among them are Plowboy Medders and Harold, two fellows who ran the bottling operation there. (In those days, every plant had its own bottling operation. The idea of over-the-road trucking of products had not yet arrived.)

I also remember from those days that a route salesman named Bobby Williams worked Rockmart. He was a big, good looking guy. His helper was a man named Hugh Hardison. Hugh's father was a local railroad detective. Hugh had just gotten out of the Navy and was getting ready to go play football at Georgia Tech. Hugh was the helper, I was the rider of the routes, and Williams was the salesman. Williams was, of course, our boss for the day. In subsequent years, Williams left the Coca-Cola business and joined the Georgia State Patrol. He was later promoted to captain and retired somewhere in South Georgia. Hugh Hardison, interestingly enough, became a state patrolman as well. Subsequently, he became the head of the whole Georgia State Patrol and was Bobby William's boss. But that was the way things happened in those days.

This is a picture of the old Cedartown plant which was located on Main Street.

Cartersville

In all of this discussion, it is probably apparent that I have said little or nothing about Cartersville. There's a reason for that, and it's the subject of a long story. I'd like to relate that story now.

In the early 1920's, when my grandfather was beginning to acquire Cedartown, Carrollton, and Cartersville, he did so in connection with Mr. Ed Cole. (Actually, his name was E. Dargen Cole, but everyone called him "Ed.") Mr. Cole died in 1929, so I never knew him. However, Mr. Cole and my grandfather, and subsequently my father and my uncle, all worked together. All through the 1930's, 40's and 50's after Mr. Cole died, my father looked after the Cartersville plant, as well as his ongoing duties running the Rome plant. Alfred Lee looked after Cedartown, Carrollton, and when we acquired Fort Valley, that plant as well. Dalton was under Clarence Archer's operation, and this was the way things were arranged until the late 1950's.

In the late 1950's, my dad was still running Cartersville, to some degree, and also Rome. Now when I say "to some degree," it is because Mr. Cole had a son named Dargan, who was some years older than me. Dargan had been a navy pilot during World War II. However, he was not a typical, hardworking, up-at-5:00-in-the-morning Coca-Cola bottler. He was a member of the Piedmont Driving Club in Atlanta, and he had a great interest in golf.

Perhaps as a result of Dargan's leisure activities—or just because he ran a lousy operation—Dargan and Alfred had a personality clash. Their difference in personalities was acceptable as long as my dad went there once a week to pay the bills and instruct Dargan what to do. However, my dad was getting on up in years, and he soon had his first brush with heart disease. Soon, he was unable to look after

Cartersville. Alfred Lee was a very energetic fellow, and so he began to look over the plant there. But Dargan continued to alienate him. I had basically been forbidden to go to Cartersville because they didn't want me over there clashing with Dargan. And I followed their wishes—simply because I didn't know to do any differently.

One day in 1959, Alfred and Daddy finally said, "That's it Dargan." So Alfred Lee and I went over there one day, and Alfred did all of the talking. He said, "Dargan, you have to do either one of three things. Either we're going to buy you out right now, or you're going to buy us out right now, or you're going to walk out of this plant and never going to walk back in the door again. We're not going to be a part of an operation like this. You make your choice." Alfred told him that we would continue paying his dividends and his salary for six months or a year. Dargan said that would suit him just fine—he didn't like to work anyway. He picked up his things and left. We never saw Dargan in the office again.

Robert Redden's version of the Cartersville Coca-Cola Plant. We expanded it twice after this picture was drawn.

The immediate question on everyone's mind was who the successor to Dargan would be. Before he left, Dargan had asked Alfred that very question. Alfred simply turned to me and replied, "Frank is." I knew nothing about Cartersville and I knew even less about the people there. I knew Hugh Smith and that was the end of it. I then began spending most of my time in Cartersville. All through the 1960's, I went to Carrollton, Cedartown, and Dalton occasionally, but from 1959 to about 1966, my time was spent primarily in Cartersville.

Some of the wonderful people I remember from that town were Hugh Smith, who ran the plant; Wayne Swanson, the route supervisor; Jack Smith; Ernest Kukyndahl; Paul Roebuck, who ran the filler; and Hubert Tidwell, the refrigeration man. Hubert later ran the filler and was production manager.

In the later years, Katie Chadwick was the bookkeeper and one of the finest ladies I have ever known. In most operations that we had, the men were all very young, aggressive people and there were all rather raunchy. In their conversations they used a good bit of profanity, but not when Katie was in the office. Under Wayne Swanson and Katie, Cartersville was the cleanest and most organized plant run in history, as far as I know. There were absolutely no off color stories or anything of that nature. It was just a wonderful place to be.

It seems that in the very early 1950's, Cartersville Coca-Cola Bottling was having a bit of a small dispute with Atlanta Coca-Cola. The territories of the original franchises were very specifically spelled out. In many cases, the franchise boundary lines were referenced to railroad tracks or city limits because those were the definitive measures of the day. It was not drawn out like a plot.

In the Cartersville situation, Cartersville worked the town of Acworth as described by the old city limits. These limits were roughly described as being a circle drawn exactly one mile in radius around the city hall, as I recall. Nevertheless, this one mile radius circle passed through what was then the old U.S. 41 Highway. There was a dispute about where the territory lines lay.

Hugh Smith, a man of great honor and integrity, went to Atlanta with Alfred Lee and a few others. Their purpose was to argue the situation with L.F. Montgomery and Elmer Barton. L.F. was the owner of the Atlanta Coca-Cola operation. The operation consisted of eight plants—Griffin, Gainesville, and others. Elmer Barton was an in-law and the general manager.

There was apparently a huge discussion between the men—almost a fist fight—over one grocery store that was sitting right on the boundary of the old city limit line. They finally agreed that the territory line would be dependent on which side of the little store the Coca-Cola cooler sat. If it sat on the side towards Atlanta, then it would be Atlanta's store. If the cooler were placed on the Cartersville side of the store, then it would be Cartersville's store. Of course, none of the Atlanta people knew where the cooler sat, or even really where the store was located. But Hugh Smith, a hands-on sales manager at the time, knew exactly where the cooler was. So on the way back to Cartersville from Atlanta, Hugh persuaded Alfred to go back through Acworth and drop him off for a few minutes while he went in and explained to the store manager. He said that they were good friends and he was going to move the cooler to the other side of the store. Thus, the store became Cartersville territory for the rest of the time.

Hugh was not a marketing man and was never very demanding of his people. I always knew he would be where he was supposed to be. He and Wayne Swanson were two of the most honest people I've ever known in my life. Hugh was a product of the old school; he would get up in the morning and get the trucks out. I remember he, Alfred, and Daddy particularly never did understand why a route had to be changed. Once it had been set, it was pretty much set in concrete, and the idea of changing a route, regardless of the growth in a particular community, was a very painful thing for them to change. I guess being younger and from a different generation, I used to tell my managers that if they weren't changing their routes every month or so, they were behind. Nothing was that static. I think it was a matter of age, timing, and generation gaps that affected these sorts of things.

Many very interesting happenings took place in Cartersville in the late 1960's as the industrial expansion of North Georgia began full speed. The mayor of Cartersville, Charlie Cowan, was a rather aggressive fellow, as was the Bartow County Manager, Griffin Smith. These two gentlemen embarked an industrial growth program that paid great dividends. Of course, Cartersville was on the main road from Chattanooga to Atlanta in those days, which was Highway 41. Because of the city's prime location, many industrial organizations began to look at Cartersville with a great deal of interest—as did Union Carbide, which came to town during this time. Union Carbide was a plastic manufacturing operation.

As the "Soaring Sixties" drew to a close, we had really begun to expand our business, having bought the Valdosta plant, acquiring a union, selling cans and ten and thirty two ounce returnables, and producing with the pre-mix. Times were changing. My father was not in bad health, but he wasn't in good health, either. So in the late 1960's and early 1970's, Mike and Al began to assume more leadership. Mike had finished his tour in Vietnam as a Marine Corp Captain. I'm not sure if he and his wife, Patty, had been married by this time or not, but Al of course was married and may have had a child or two by this time.

Valdosta

As mentioned earlier, we had bought the Coca-Cola plant in Valdosta in 1965. The process of taking over the Valdosta Plant was most interesting. I still remember several people from Valdosta, such as Lester Poole, Harry Stewart, Calvin Graham, and Clyde Armstrong. I also remember Arminda Newcome, who subsequently married a man named Morrison.

When we bought the Valdosta plant it had an interesting philosophy about its trucking and loading operation. The folks down there thought it was a waste of time for route salesmen to come in and load the trucks. It turned out that several of the route salesmen down there never drove their own trucks and never touched the first case. They had a black helper who handled the cases and drove the truck, leaving the salesman to do a little reshuffling of the displays and to freshen up this and that. Occasionally, the salesmen would load the vending machines and collect the money. The way the system worked was that each salesman had two trucks, he drove one truck and sold the Coca-Cola off of it while the second truck was in the plant being loaded as the day went on. The result of this was when he got back in the afternoon, his tomorrow truck was already sitting there loaded and ready for him to go. Obviously this required twice as many trucks as we felt were necessary.

One of the first things we did immediately was to do away with this whole system of doing things. Since there were about ten routes in Valdosta, we sold all but the ten best trucks and went on about our business. Several of the trucks in Valdosta were still what we referred to in those days as "deck trucks."

We had a lot of work to do in Valdosta because the machinery was almost antique. Mr. Harbour, the original owner, had three sons and three daughters. When he died, he left the Coca-Cola business intact to these six siblings. He took each sixth, and divided it into ninety percent and ten percent. He gave each spouse ten percent of one sixth and the child ninety percent of one sixth.

This is what the Valdosta Coca-Cola plant looked like according to Robert Redden.

When we began our negotiations, the only ones remaining of the original twelve were in-laws. One of the son-in-laws, Bill Warwick was the manager of the plant. Bill was a very good man, but he was hamstrung by his in-laws. His wife, one of the natural children, had long since died. All three of the males were dead, and the remaining two widows had remarried. It was the biggest mess. None of the family believed in doing anything. There were no dividends, and because the directors' fees were so high, there were no earnings. Their great compensation came when they have board meetings once a month and give everyone a director's fee just for showing up.

Of course, with business being run this way, the plant made very little earnings. It was a strange scene. But that goes to highlight how the Coca-Cola business was operated in the early days. Someone once said—brightly, in my opinion—that how the

Coca-Cola industry survived its early days is certainly a testimony to the greatness of the product itself.

Harvard, Unions

One of the great things that happened to me in those days was the opportunity to go to Harvard. This was the result of efforts by Paul Austin, who was president of Coca-Cola at the time.

Paul was tall, good-looking guy—an ex-PT boat skipper during World War II and a big Harvard fan. Paul was a heavy drinker who later developed Parkinson's disease. He thought that the average Coca-Cola bottler was woefully uneducated, and he was right. So what he did was to start a graduate school, so to speak, in connection with Harvard University. Because Paul was interested in attracting younger bottlers to the program, I was one of the bottlers selected to go. He invited several other bottlers to attend as well, such as Carl Navarre and Crawford Johnson. Don Keough was asked to come because the Coca-Cola Company had just bought out Duncan Foods and Don was the rising young executive with that company. He wanted Don to learn the Coca-Cola business.

I met many people for the first time up at Harvard, such as Preacher Franklin and Jack Lupton and Crawford Johnson (better known as Trey). George Overend was teaching there at the time. We attended three distinct courses: People Management, Marketing Management, and Money Management. The money management course was on the principles of cost accounting—it was the first time any of us had heard of such a thing because we weren't accountants. The theories that I learned there have stood me in a great stead ever since. I learned more in those weeks at Harvard than I had learned in all of my college classes. Probably one of the greatest parts of the experience was meeting people in the industry such as Charley Wallace, Don Keough, and others—people who went on to run Coca-Cola in the later days. Altogether, it an enormously satisfying and a very productive experience.

Along about this time, the Rome plant began to be organized into a union. It was quite a shock for all of us to be petitioned for a union election. Of course, our local lawyers immediately recommended that we contact some lawyers from Atlanta. It was typical of the times—unions were just popping up everywhere. Rome became quite a highly organized union town in no time at all; not only was GE organized, but so were Inland Container and most of the bigger mills and industries.

Our plant got organized because we had poor people management practices going on in Rome. A manager could afford to be paternalistic in a small town like Cartersville or maybe even Dalton, a notoriously anti-union town, but Rome was a different story. The idea of top management "knowing what was best for everyone" just didn't fly in these modern '60's. Later on, some of the men told me that it was primarily because of some of the middle management that they felt like they couldn't get a fair hearing from Alfred Lee and Daddy.

We were surprised that our workers did not want to be involved with the Teamsters Union, and when we started talking to the lawyers, they were amazed as well. The Communications Workers of America was an incredibly smart organization. Its members were bright, intelligent, and reasonable. Nevertheless, we went into the election and lost, and the next thing we knew we had a union. Interestingly enough, as soon as we begin the negotiations, the lawyers asked me to be the negotiator because they thought that Alfred and Willie were too close to the situation. Jack Rogers, our lawyer, would sit down with me every night and say, "Here's what they're going to tell you..." and then he would tell me what that would really mean. They were all kinds of sophisticated arguments that I didn't understand. But Jack led me through, and we got a three year contract the first time and were on our way.

I later negotiated for three or four more contracts because the philosophy was that I did not have enough power to make weighty decisions. I could only say that we would try and that I thought we could sell such-and-such idea. But I always had the excuse of saying I needed to take the idea back to Alfred Lee and my Dad. Of course, they always had the ability to reply, "But you know we have to take this to our membership." All we were doing was creating a level playing field. I certainly learned a lot from those years of negotiating labor contracts.

There's an interesting story from the mid 1970's about the last contract I negotiated. Due to some terrible impasse that has since faded into history, we thought we were going to have a strike. The expiration date on our previous contract was only a few short days away, and we were having some serious difficulties getting a new one arranged. Fortunately, though, we thought to ask T'Tie Tolbert or one of our home deliverymen to deliver about forty cases of Coca-Cola's to daddy's house, my house, Alfred's, Lloyd's, and Virginia's house. It sent shock waves throughout the work force to see us apparently preparing for a strike. The upshot, however, was that negotiations got much easier and we were then able to conclude a contract without missing a day. In fact, we never had a strike at all.

One of the gentlemen I negotiated with in the early days was the president of the Communications Workers. He was named Buddy Higgins. A major difficulty with my dealings with Buddy was the need to educate him in the soft drink business. He knew hardly anything about it. But Buddy always was and remains to be a very fine and honorable man. He and I found ourselves in situations in which it was necessary to "plea the Fifth" from time to time, but Buddy never told me anything that I later found out to be a lie. I never told him a lie, either.

Buddy and I could talk at night on the telephone and prearrange our negotiations, which we would then reenact in "official" business meetings the next day. Sometimes, Buddy would tell me, "Frank, what you're asking for, I just can't deliver, they just won't go for it." Then I would tell him I was going to protest like the devil, but he could have his side in the end. Needless to say, much of the negotiating was done outside the negotiating table. As I said earlier, it was very much a learning experience. I was just glad that we were able to change our policies, change our philosophies, and upgrade the other six plants.

Whatever happened in Rome, it was almost guaranteed that we were going to better it in the other plants. To some degree, it was very frustrating to the Rome fellows. They knew that whatever they negotiated in Rome, the folks in Cartersville and Dalton were going to get just a little bit better. As a result, we removed any possible further organization from the other plants. But we did learn a great deal about how to work with people.

Some of the other enjoyable memories I have from those days involve Tommy Matthews of Olin Mathison Chemical Company. In the earlier days of the industry, we had created our carbonated water by buying large blocks of dry ice and placing them in great pressurized containers that looked like torpedoes. The ice would melt over a period of a week to ten days, and then we would mix the liquid CO_2 in the carbonator to become the fizz in the Coca-Colas. In later years, however, CO_2 was delivered under pressure in great refrigerated tanks. We elected to do all of our business with Olin Mathison Chemical Company, and Tommy Matthews was the fellow who engineered the deal. Our group of plants, which by that time numbered seven, became one of his largest accounts. We were second only to the Atlanta chain in size. We were later on to use this difference to our advantage, but that's another story.

Mr. John Olin, executive of both Olin Mathison Chemical Company and Winchester Rifle Company, was still living in those days. Mr. Olin was great hunter and dog lover. He had farms in Georgia and Illinois, and he called them both "Nilo" (which is "Olin" spelled backwards). Once a year, Tommy Matthews would invite me, Alfred Lee, and later on Mike and Al, to go up to the Illinois farm for a hunting trip. Mr. Olin's company plane would come pick us up. I remember that Elmo Barton, part of the Atlanta Coca-Cola group, went with us one time, and we had a lot of fun. The Olins had Labrador Retrievers and all kinds of dogs that would hunt the ducks and quail that we would shoot. I remember one very famous dog at Nilo Farms. His name was King Buck, and he was a Labrador retriever. He became the only dog ever to be put on a duck stamp. When King Buck died, he was buried up there on the Nilo Farms. He was buried better than Robert E. Lee!

The 1970s

In the 1930's and 1940's, it had seemed that things were never going to change. But by the time the 1960's and 1970's came along, people began to realize that change was inevitable. They also began to think about how quickly things were going to change and how they could prepare themselves for it.

One of the most pervasive changes that was coming along in our business was the philosophy of cooperative advertising. Prior to the 1970's, the idea of cooperative advertising had meant that the Coca-Cola Company would pay for part of our newspaper or radio ads. We would agree on a budget at the beginning of the year for newspaper and radio ads. Then, the Coca-Cola Company would look at our sales and allocate us so much per gallon to be spent on advertising. We were required to prove that we were going to spend our share. This, of course, was an unhandy way of doing business. Usually, we would just say to the Coca-Cola Company, "Look, you know us, we know you. We're up here in Rome and you know what we spend. We have these high per capita plants, 5 out of the top ten per capita plants in the country. We are not only going to spend what you're asking us to get our full cooperation from you, but we are going to spend more than that. Just allow us our advertising, give us our money, give us the discount, and forget about it." And that was that. We had an account which paid us five cents for every gallon of Coca-Cola we produced, and we were to spend it on signs, stickers, and posters for promotion of the product.

A major facet of cooperative advertising came along when several major supermarket chains tired of dealing with a different bottler for each of their different stores. Kroger, Winn Dixie, and others said, in effect, "We want the Coca-Cola Company to tell us that on the 4th of July, the Coca-Cola bottlers of the state of Georgia will have such and such a deal." The

Coca-Cola Industry was, for the most part, divided up between Rome and Atlanta. As I recall, together we controlled more or less fifty-four percent of the state's total volume. Jim Coffey, secretary of the Georgia Council of Bottlers of Coca-Cola, organized the logistics of the Kroger project. He would go the Kroger Company and set up a deal—for example, a Labor Day special—for which the case price would be set at an amount we had all agreed upon previously. Then, he would send out notices to the various bottlers and tell them that the deal had been cut. He would report that we should reimburse the Kroger Company through the Georgia Council of Coca-Cola Bottlers for the discounted price. The way we did it in Rome was to sell the full price to the grocery stores. That way, neither the store people who signed the ticket nor the salesman who did the invoices would be fully aware of Kroger's special discount. A check would be written to the Georgia Council of Bottlers of Coca-Cola for the amount of cases, which Jim Coffey would take back to the Kroger store after the sale. All in all, the system worked out pretty well.

Another major factor in the cooperative advertising discussion was the strong advent of television. Television became the major factor in advertising. Whereas newspapers and radio had previously served as our major media, television was now "where it was at."

We began to wonder how we would allocate the costs of a television ad. The costs were allocated by some very sophisticated population demographics for the coverage of Atlanta channels 2, 5, and 11. Chattanooga had its own television station, Rome, of course, had none. We didn't know when or what the ads were going to be, and we had little input into what we thought was desirable. It was probably for the best since we had no television expertise. Neither did Atlanta, who gained what knowledge they could out of necessity and quickly became the experts. Great discussions ensued as to how many television ads we should buy and what kind of ads were best. I can still hear the arguments now. All the older bottlers would say the ads were childish and no good; they thought all the ads needed to say was "Coca-Cola refreshes." But there was a new generation of viewers out there, and even those of us who were 40 or 50 were in no place to judge what made good television. While some of the ads didn't necessarily appeal to me either, for the most part they were very successful. Who could ever forget, "Mean Joe Green" or "I'd Like To Buy The World A Coke"? It's very interesting that I have just noticed that The Coca-Cola Company is planning on bringing these particular commercials back. Evidently time doesn't change everything.

The Georgia Welcome Stations were another interesting factor to deal with in cooperative advertising. The welcome stations were major centers located very close to the state line on the interstate highways. People who came into the state would stop, ask directions, and receive a welcome to Georgia. The stations became immensely popular. There were nine stations, as I recall, and they were operated by the Georgia Department of Industry, Trade, and Tourism (then the Georgia Department of Industry and Trade). The Georgia Council of Bottlers of Coca-Cola gave a free Coca-Cola and the peanut industry gave a bag of peanuts to everyone who stopped there. There was a small assessment to each of approximately 52 bottlers around the state. Then the serving bottlers would be reimbursed for providing the pre-mix.

As time passed, the project became a huge expense. Valdosta, for example, was giving away hundreds of tanks of Coca-Cola per month. Traffic flow on the interstates began to increase, and when people found out they could get free Coca-Cola and peanuts at the welcome stations...well, they just covered those places up. Finally, we had to get out of it. Coca-Cola replaced the program with vending machines, which is how the welcome stations are serviced to this day. But that was another example of how bottlers across the state had to cooperate with one another. The Kroger specials, the television ads, the welcome stations—all these were little tacks in the wood that began to lead to the eventual selling of franchises and the consolidation of plants.

Al Parsons, Carrolton; Hugh Smith, Cartersville; me and Clarence Archer at Roselawn in Cartersville in late 1970s

Gasoline stations were big business in the 1970's. One of the first marketing schemes that was used to get cartons of Coca-Cola's into the service stations was by placing carton racks in front of the service stations. As patrons stopped to buy gas on their way home, they could buy a carton of Coca-Cola and turn in their empty bottles. This was big business. One of the measures of how good an operator or salesman was at the time was how well he kept his carton racks full and rotated.

Also in these days, pre-mix vending frequently became a replacement for post-mix vending. The difference between pre-mix and post-mix vending was very simple. In post-mix, which was the old concept, syrup was dispensed into a cup. Carbonated water was added later or perhaps even at the same time. Sanitation was not necessarily important because the carbonation kept the carbonated water lines clean. The syrup wasn't carbonated, so it didn't foam. However, in the pre-mix vending, the syrup and carbonated water were mixed before bottling. There could not be one speck of dirt because dirt tended to make the water foam when there was syrup in it. No matter how clean the line was by normal standards, the slightest trace of dirt would make the drink foam.

One of the early innovators of the pre-mix system was a gentleman named Carl Navarre. Carl was the founder of the Dixie Narco Company, a little cooler manufacturing plant up in Chattanooga. He also had a plant in West Virginia, and he later went on to buy Miami Coca-Cola. Among other things, Carl was a world-class bone fisherman who owned a lodge in The Keys named "Cheeka Lodge."

The reason we began to deal with pre-mix vending was that it was a necessary move to make in our attempts to capture Union Carbide, the newest industry in Cartersville's business. Union Carbide was a plastic manufacturing plant, and its owners refused to have any sort of glass in their plant. We introduced in that mill the first pre-mix vending machine in our area—perhaps even in the state of Georgia. The idea was imperfect at best and required a lot of hand holding. I became the only person who was interested in it. I would go down to Cartersville a couple of times a week to make sure the system was sanitized. Eventually, we were able to train some people to help out with the sanitation so I didn't have to go down quite so frequently.

It is interesting that the person who became our first pre-mix expert was Dargan Cole III. Dargan is now a stockbroker in Atlanta. He is a fine young man who worked for us in the summers and became our pre-mix expert. As the 1960's developed, pre-mix vending became a rather large portion of our vending mix.

Another factor in our operation in those days was a technique called "full service" (which, by the way, is still in operation). It is a technique by which a mill of some size would be serviced by one man. The Lindale Mill in Rome, which probably housed 40 or 50 of our vending machines, was an example of one such mill. Full service was an all day, everyday job. The technician would do nothing but go around filling the machines and collecting the money from them.

The way the system worked was that after the money was collected from the machines, it would be deposited in the bank. At the end of the month, we would send the Lindale manager a check for his portion of the total take, which was perhaps 15-20%. In reality, it was a very lucrative and labor intensive sort of business. We were responsible for filling and servicing every machine, bringing in all the bottles, and counting the money. We had two girls who did nothing but count nickels, dimes, and quarters. Full service vending became quite a big business.

A great memory of mine from those days was the Vince Dooley Bulldog Show. It was sponsored by the Georgia Coca-Cola Group and run by a marvelous gentleman named Loren Smith. Loren was and remains to this day the sideline color man for the University of Georgia football games. The University, on Sundays, would sponsor a television show called "The Georgia Football Show." It was a commentary and replay of the previous Saturday's football game by head coach Vince Dooley. Buddy Sams over in Athens (which, of course, is where the University of Georgia is located) was a little hesitant to be the spokesman for the show.

In 1980, when Georgia won the national championship by defeating Notre Dame in the Sugar Bowl, the show became a very valuable commodity to us. Pepsi Cola soon began to express an interest in the program, and so the University wanted to charge us more. Buddy Sams, the Athens bottler, didn't want to represent the other Georgia bottlers in the negotiations with UGA because he feared the rest of us might think he was trying to increase his influence in his territory. But the rest of us across the state saw it as a state-wide project, not as a local project, and somehow or another I ended up as being a little bit of the advocate for the bottlers and for Loren Smith. I always felt I had to do this because Richard Horsey, then General Manager of Atlanta was a big Georgia Tech fan and just didn't have any use for the University of Georgia. This setup worked very well for many years.

Sometime in the mid to late 1970's, Atlanta Coca-Cola sold out. It was a traumatic time. I don't know the exact circumstances behind it, but I am aware that Arthur Montgomery and his brother George, the major stockholders in Atlanta Coca-Cola, predicted several years prior to the transaction that the business would run into some problems in the future. It was rumored that some foreign oil industries were interested in buying Atlanta Coca-Cola. The Coca-Cola Company, knowing that it would be dangerous to sell the home of the industry to an outsider, bought out Atlanta before that could happen. The nominal manager the plant was Richard Horsey. Formerly Arthur Montgomery's brother-in-law, Richard was a small, balding fellow of great intelligence. He was almost a genius. I had great regard for Richard, although he was a little bit fiery and we had a couple of run-ins. Richard spoke for Atlanta Coca-Cola and Alfred, my dad, and I spoke for Rome. There was a good cooperative feeling between us, and we worked well together.

In the ever-changing scene of the 1970's there was a fellow in Carrollton named Aubrey Jones. He had been an Air Force pilot during World War II, but in later years he drifted into the financial end of the Air Force and became an accountant. Alfred Lee hired Aubrey as our controller, except we didn't call the position by that term in those days. He devised a much simpler system for checking up.

Unfortunately, however, Aubrey and my father didn't get along very well. Daddy, being of the old school, didn't want to change anything—particularly anything that had to do with accounting. My father didn't foresee that the advent of sales tax collection would change in our accounting needs. We went through a rather difficult situation with the sales tax division of the Georgia Department of Revenue. They claimed after performing an audit that we had grossly understated our payment of sales tax. They were probably correct. Alfred Lee and I went down to Atlanta and cut a deal with them, saying that we didn't know how much we had undercharged and we didn't know how much we should be fined. But we offered them a figure that we could live with if they could, which they accepted. Implicit in that settlement, of course, was the agreement that we would correct our accounting system so that we could accurately check the sales tax.

The advent of the Computer Age was fast approaching, but computerization was a frightening challenge that no one wanted to tackle. However, we found computers being practically forced upon us for numerous reasons. It was very difficult to get all the salesmen, all the time, to write down which dealers had sales tax numbers and which ones didn't.

By this time, we were dealing with many, many products in many different sizes: cans, non-returnables, premix syrup, postmix syrup, packages, 32 ounce sizes, and different flavors. We needed a better method for finding out what a store was selling. For example, if a store was selling nothing but Coca-

Cola, we could determine very quickly if we were missing some bets by not selling Sprite. We tried for many years to have our route salesmen carry a little book in which they recorded their number of sales to each account, but it never did work. The information was often recorded in the afternoon when a man had finished his route. His memory was faulty, and he wrote the information quickly. Recording the transactions was not a fun thing to do, and the accounts rarely balanced. When we raised the issue to our salesmen that we weren't getting sufficient records from them, they would perhaps begin to sit down in the afternoons and record what they had delivered during that entire day. But of course, the figures never balanced up. Computers were headed our way.

In the late 1970's, Aubrey Jones and George Perry, who worked for our CPA, discovered a company in North Carolina that might solve our problem. Along with some other bottlers, we formed a cooperative venture to own a hand held, computerized check-in system. We were among the first to use the system, and it worked out fine. The way that the system worked was that our salesmen would carry the computer in the store with them and pull out the cash or charge ticket. The computer automatically knew whether it was required to add sales tax or not. Given that our men punched in their information accurately, we were able to print out a record of their deliveries every day. It was, in effect, a copy of the settlement sheet. In today's world, this system probably seems simple and perhaps even archaic. But in those days, it was very innovative, very unique, and very original.

Mike and Al were fully on the scene in those days, and the three of us spent a lot of time going to Valdosta and Fort Valley. We would head out early in the morning, the three of us in one car, stopping in Cedartown a few minutes for Al. Then we'd swing to Carrollton for a few minutes for Mike, head on down to Fort Valley, and end up in Valdosta. We'd stay at the

King of the Road Motel. I must say that we had some mighty good times down there eating steak and drinking liquor, charging it to the company, and staying in the motel. It was a lot of fun—one of the highlights of the decade.

Another very innovative thing that we did in those days was to buy an airplane. Mike, Al, and I were spending a ridiculous amount of time in an automobile. I was still more or less overseeing the Valdosta plant and in the process of turning it over to Mike, Al was running Cedartown and Fort Valley, and Mike was heading up Carrollton. We saw that we were denying our availability to the other operations. So in 1976 we decided to buy an airplane.

The first airplane that we bought was a Cessna 421, a piston driven airplane that was pressurized. We hired a fellow named Pete Blevins to fly it. (I had been flying since 1951, but I stopped when I had children.) Pete was a gentleman of the first order and a lot of fun to be around. Pete had his instructor's license, so I asked him to carry me up so I could finish what I had started back in 1951. I soon got my license, and later Mike did too. We both subsequently became multi-engine rated. Later, we traded the Cessna 421 for a King Air C-90. Then, we traded this for a King Air B-100. Under IRS direction, we developed a method so that we could use the plane for our own personal use, provided that we paid the holding company which bought and owned it. We had to pay a substantial fee per hour, but it still was better than flying on the airlines. But all of these airplanes were sold, of course, when the business was sold in 1986. The only word of advice that I have to anyone contemplating getting in the airplane business is to get ready—it is the single most expensive venture a person can undertake. But it sure is a lot of fun.

This is the last airplane we had. It was a King Air BE100 that we bought in 1983. Wonderful airplane that seated 12 people.

Somewhere in the mid to late 1970's, we decided to shut down Cartersville. Because of production problems, we simply couldn't afford to buy the kind of equipment their facilities required. It became clear that we were going to have to centralize our production facilities. In 1977, we broke ground on a new plant—now the plant on 27 South.

The New Rome Plant

Mr. Willie-1976 at the new plant in Rome

The new plant was a major undertaking. Alfred Lee took it upon himself to build that plant, and he did. There was no question about it. He hired Jack Frost, a one-time architect who had also worked at the Rome Housing Authority. All of us had advice, consulting sessions, and arguments about what was going to go where. I think a prime argument between

Mike, Al, and I occurred when we tried to gently recommend to Alfred Lee that production and sales had two separate functions and therefore ought to be separated physically. This didn't happen primarily due to financial considerations. We didn't have enough room to build two buildings in Rome—one to be Rome's sales center, and one to be our joint production. The way it worked out, Rome owned the production facility and in effect sold products to Valdosta, Cartersville, and everyone else.

By the time we finished the plant, which took about a year and a half to complete, we had all brand new machinery. We had visited many plants around the Southeast looking at production facilities. We were trying to decide what the best equipment was and what the best layout for a plant was. But we soon came to the conclusion that it didn't make any difference how well we built our plant—the day we started bottling was the day our machinery became obsolete. Technology was simply changing at a very

At the 1976 ground breaking of the new plant. Left to right: my Father, Willie Barron, Al Barron my cousin, Me, Uncle Alfred Lee, and Mike Barron my cousin.

rapid pace. Nonetheless, there were two elements to our plant that were rather unique. First, the bottling room itself had absolutely no columns in it. It was to be free-span 120 feet. Of course, this was a more expensive way to build because the roof beams had to be larger. However, it gave us total freedom to move our machinery around. New equipment for labeling, new equipment for dating, and so many other different products were coming along in those days, but all we had to do was move things around because we had all that open space.

The second innovation was the way the plant was designed to house our equipment. In most plants, equipment such as air compressors, refrigeration compressors, air conditioning, and boilers were in the basement. Removing or replacing the machines was a major operation which sometimes involved cutting a hole in the floor. Our solution to this problem was that we built a berm out in front of our new plant. The bottling facility looked to be one story if a person were

This picture was drawn later by Robert Redden. It's the new plant in Rome on Hwy. 27 South.

to look at it from the road, but if he walked over towards the plant, he would soon see a complete platform beneath the ground level. We could just drive a truck into the berm, haul the old equipment out, and haul the new equipment in. It was a model of efficiency in materials handling for its day.

We started bottling in the new plant in 1977, as I recall. My father died later on that year. Some of the reasons why we left 5th Avenue had to do with traffic and many other things. Right before we left, someone had written an article in a bottler magazine of some description, writing about a particular plant that was supposedly the oldest existing Coca-Cola plant in the same location. However, we did some research and came to the conclusion that we were the oldest existing Coca-Cola plant still in operation in the original location.

After we moved out to the new bottling operation, Alfred decided that we needed to have our own can line. We bought a small can line and put it in the old plant. I think it ran something like 460 cans a minute, which was an incredibly fast speed in the case of bottles. But in the case of cans, later on the speeds got up to 1200 cans per minute. For all I know, some became even faster than that! We had to put a small can plant up there in Rome in 1978 so that technically, we were still bottling in the original location. As I said in the beginning, we thought that we were the sixth oldest plant, but the other five and since moved probably two or three times. Therefore, we did have the distinction at one time of being the oldest plant still in operation in the same location.

One of the reasons that we moved was because of the little street on North 5th Avenue that ran behind the plant. The street was directly behind the drive-in windows of the National City Bank and also behind the Atlanta Gas Light Company. The resultant traffic jams from all of this congestion were just horrendous. In addition, we had simply outgrown the North 5th Avenue plant.

We had acquired too many acres of the land out on the 27 South location. Eventually we sold a few of these acres. In fact, at a later time, Rome built its own warehouse and office across the street. The original plant was downsized to a production facility. Because products were indeed just hauled across the street to the Rome facility, the plant not only physically, but also financially changed hands from Rome Coca-Cola Bottling Company to Rome Distribution Warehouse Center.

My father died in October of 1977. His last three or four years were not productive ones, and it was not a very happy time for him or anyone. Dad was more or less homebound for the last year, so he had a nurse stay with him during his last few months. What I remember most about my father was that he was probably the single most respected Coca-Cola man in the country. Time and time again, people have told me how much they admired him. Someone even wrote a praising editorial about him in The Coca-Cola Bottling Magazine. He was quite a man and certainly taught me almost everything I know.

At the time of his funeral, my mother had broken her leg, having fallen in the yard one night as she was walking over to my house. Anne and I were having a dinner party, and I remember that Paul and Candy Ferguson were among the guests. We kept hearing what we thought was a sheep crying out in the yard. Finally, we got up to go look, and it was mother. After she was yelling for someone to come pick her up, Paul immediately diagnosed her broken leg.

My Father's funeral was held at First Baptist Church, and I can remember having to go through the back door with my family because Mother was still in a wheelchair and couldn't go down the aisle. Of course, Alfred Lee, Jane, Virginia and Lloyd with their children, and Anne and me and our children were all there. It was without a doubt the largest funeral I have ever seen. The police had to block off 4th Avenue because the traffic was so heavy. The church was totally packed, and there were even people standing out on the streets. It was a marvelous tribute to a man who had meant so much to the Coca-Cola business and to Rome itself.

Intrabrand Competition Act, Consolidation and Saccharine Ban

Clearly, the 1970's were years of many, many changes for me—not only personally, but in the business as well. Anne, I, Frank, III and Rebekah had moved in 1970 to Horseleg Creek Road, the house where I had grown up. That was also the era of the Federal Trade Commission challenge.

Sometime in early 1977 or 1978, the Federal Trade Commission suddenly issued a declaration that exclusive franchises, such as bottling franchises, were illegal. Their theory was that a Chattanooga bottler, for example, couldn't be denied the right to sell to a supermarket chain in Rome. The contention of the bottlers, however, was that they had vast amounts of money invested in what was called "bottle float"—that is, the amount of bottles that they owned. If Atlanta came to Rome and sold Coca-Cola's for a cheaper price, then Atlanta would pick up the empty bottles and, theoretically, take all of our empty bottles back to Atlanta. Another problem was that some of the larger Coca-Cola plants had the ability to produce a bit cheaper, so that if Atlanta wanted to come in and do business with all of the Kroger's, they would come in and take away all the A & P's and the Piggly Wiggly's as well. This would take away all of our high volume accounts and make the smaller ones—the doctor's accounts and accounts in other various office buildings—even more expensive than they already were to handle.

The FTC probably had a good point on paper. The political reality, however, was that in those days there were probably somewhere between eight and nine hundred individual Coca-Cola bottling plants, plus an equal amount of other plants, scattered throughout the United States. When the Federal Trade Commission made their ruling, the entire bottling community went up in arms. The Coca-Cola Company immediately jumped out and said that they would support the bottlers, helping to finance whatever effort we jointly thought was wise. Pepsi Cola Company was somewhat slow to join the fight. However, after pressures from their own bottlers they subsequently joined us. The National Soft Drink Association, then headed by Tom Baker and Dwight Reed, planned several legal strategies to combat the FTC's ruling—strategies too complex for the average bottler to understand. The second strategy, however—and the one which ultimately worked—was a legislative one.

President Jimmy Carter, a Georgia native, was considered to be a very close friend to the Coca-Cola Company. He was, therefore, regarded as our great asset. As there was probably not a single legislator in the country who did not know his Coca-Cola, Pepsi-Cola, or other bottler personally, an enormous effort was made to bombard the legislators in Washington. The primary legislation was introduced by then Senator Birch Bayh of Indiana. Senator Bayh was a very close friend of a bottler from Portland, Indiana named Bob Delauter. (Mr. Delauter subsequently became president of the National Soft Drink Association.) The act that was introduced eventually became known as "The Intrabrand Competition Act." Although it took about a year and a half to get the act introduced and to get support for it, the act was overwhelmingly passed by both the House and the Senate. President Carter was advised not to sign it, but he said that he was going to sign it anyway. And he did, thus saving our bacon.

About the time our dealings with the FTC were drawing to a close, a small but fairly convincing move towards consolidation began to develop in the bottling community. Larger bottling equipment was becoming the norm, and efficiencies of production, distribution, and advertising were becoming real facts of life. As a result, some of the smaller bottling plants were being bought up by their larger competitors. The political clout that we had achieved while passing the Intrabrand Competition Act began to dissolve as local congressmen lost their personal contacts with individual bottlers.

One prevalent assumption after the passing of the Intrabrand Competition Act was that there would be substantially increased competition between the different bottling companies—for example, between Coke and Pepsi. And there was. Fortunately for us, Rome and some of our other Northwest Georgia plants had very high market shares—somewhere between eighty five and ninety percent of the entire market. Had the Federal Trade Commission come to Rome, Cartersville, Dalton, Cedartown, or Carrollton to monitor us, we probably would have been in violation of fair competition practices. They would have banned us from promoting our product for a year or so to let Pepsi gain a larger market. But we were never investigated, and so we were able to maintain those high market shares right up until the time we sold. That high market share continues until the present day.

Another very traumatic situation that had occurred in the late 1970's was the saccharine controversy. The Royal Crown Company, headquartered in Columbus, Georgia, had introduced a very innovative product called "Diet Rite." Diet Rite was a soft drink that had no sugar in it. It was flavored with saccharine. At first, most of the bottlers didn't think much of it, but it began to be a large influence as time went on. Perhaps consumers were concerned about their weight, and certainly the diabetics were interested in a sugar-free product. Nevertheless, the Coca-Cola Company soon came out with Tab. Just as Tab and Diet Rite were really becoming major factors in the market, the Food and Drug Administration banned saccharine.

Perhaps here it would be helpful to describe in more detail the reason why saccharine was banned. In the mid to late 1940's, there had been a congressman named Delaney whose wife died tragically of cancer. Congressman Delaney became a strong advocate of banning any product that contained a known carcinogen. He introduced the Delaney Clause to ban all food substances that contained even minute quantities of carcinogens.

The problem was that in 1947 or so, when the bill was introduced, the technical ability to detect carcinogens was limited to the science of the day. But by 1975, when the problem with saccharine arose, the ability to identify carcinogens was greatly enhanced. Cancer causing agents could be detected down to very minute particles. The law was clear: any substance containing any amount of carcinogens was banned, even if the quantities were so small that the chances of them causing cancer were next to impossible. Obviously, it was extremely difficult to persuade anyone to think about repealing the Delaney Clause. No one wanted to be recorded as being pro-cancer and accepting carcinogens to be sold in food products. But, on the other hand, the political pressures to allow saccharine was very great. The federal government had a dilemma on its hands, and we in the Coca-Cola industry were certainly a part of it. Of course, for many years, the legislature and judiciary kept issuing delays, moratoriums, and one year reprieves. To this day, the issue is still an open one, and I wonder if it will ever be settled.

What really saved us from our saccharine dilemma was the discovery and patent of aspartame, a product we all know now as Equal. Equal had no aftertaste and no carcinogens, and it was probably the most tested product that there has ever been. During my service on the Science Committee of the National Soft Drink Association, we were exposed to all the latest technological information on sweeteners. The problem with aspartame was that although it contained no carcinogens, it did contain an agent that was thought to excite hyperactivity in children who already suffered from hyperactivity disorders. Every now and then to this day, some people argue that there was a big cover-up involving aspartame and children with a particular sensitivity to phenylalanine. However, science has shown aspartame to be one of the most tested and safest products ever introduced. A combination of aspartame and saccharine was introduced in Tab for a while, but now Diet Coke has only aspartame in it. The controversy over artificial sweeteners is a battle which the NSDA continues to fight. I found all of this to be at its peak in 1982, when I was asked to be on the board of the National Soft Drink Association.

Soft Drink Associations

The ABCB, which was the American Bottlers of Carbonated Beverages, was the representative soft drink association in Washington D.C. It was a very old and respected organization, headed up by Tom Baker, then Dwight Reed, and subsequently others. It is now led by Will Ball, who is former secretary of the Navy.

Sometime in the late 1950's, the ABCB was renamed The National Soft Drink Association. It was managed by a board of eighteen people. In the early 1980's, I was asked to join The National Soft Drink Association (NSDA). I consider this to be one of the most prestigious boards of my civic career. The board, consisting of 18 members, served as the soft drink industry's representative in Washington D.C. Six of the board members would come from the Coca-Cola Industry, six from Pepsi-Cola, and the other six came from the occasional R.C. bottlers, 7-Up bottlers, etc. Board members of the NSDA were expected, of course, to attend meetings and serve on various committees. When I was elected, I was placed on the scientific committee as well as the convention committee. We would travel from place to place to consider various locations for conventions. Large machinery, forklift trucks, uniform salesman, bottle manufacturers, and every imaginable thing to be used in the soft drink industry would be exhibited at these conventions.

One of the interesting things about the NSDA Board was that it had a very unique way of handling expenses. Members were always reimbursed for their expenses at the three or four board meetings each year. Transportation, hotels, meals—all were covered. Board members were even encouraged to bring their wives—all expenses paid! The reason the board paid for everyone's expenses was so that smaller bottlers, who perhaps could not afford the costs of these trips, would be as well represented at meetings as the larger bottlers. Charlie Millard, the president of New York City Coca-Cola Bottling Company and one of my closest friends, could clearly afford to go to Washington any time he chose—which he did—and hire a limousine—which he did. But a small Dr. Pepper bottler from Mississippi, for example, couldn't afford such luxuries; therefore, in order to make things fair, the board decided to pay the expenses of everyone.

The NSDA was the lead lobbyist contributing to the ultimate passage of the Interbrand Competition Act, a legislative measure designed to pull The Federal Trade Commission off the soft drink industry's back during the franchise lawsuits. But that story has been better presented in earlier chapters. All in all, the NSDA was a great board. I met many people from all over The United States, many of whom remain as my close friends.

I remained on the NSDA board for two years after we had sold our business. In 1986, I even served on the NSDA's Convention Committee. It was very interesting to prepare for such large conventions as the NSDA held. We expected anywhere from 21,000 to 22,000 people in large cities such as Chicago, Atlanta, and Dallas. We would have to meet approximately one year before the annual convention was to be held so that we could look at the convention area and make plans with our consultants.

As I mentioned, I was also served as a member of the NSDA's Science Committee. It was perhaps the most interesting committee of all. Dr. Roberts, who had been a high ranking official in the Food and Drug Administration, was the staff member in charge. One topic that we studied in great detail was the topic of artificial sweeteners. We discussed products such as "left-hand sugar" and Aspartame (now known as "Equal") long before they became items of public interest, and we became very involved in the government's attempt to ban saccharine. We also went through all the scientific research that had been done about "P-K Kids," children who were extremely sensitive to the phenylalanine in Equal. Eventually, in 1986, I dropped off the board, as I was no longer actively involved in the Coca-Cola business. But everything that we studied on the NSDA Science Committee was always extremely interesting to me.

I remember a fellow from the conventions named Saul Poliak. We referred to him as the "convention guru" of the world. Saul had a small company consisting entirely of convention advisors, and it was employed by the NSDA. The six or eight of us from the convention committee would go around with one of Saul Poliak's advisors and negotiate with the convention people in that community. In some cases, our preparations were made six or eight years in advance. Then we would return one year prior to the convention to make sure that all the details had been taken care of.

When the soft drink industry came to a town, it could bring as many as 20,000-25,000 people. I think the largest convention Atlanta ever held was on the order of 23,000 people. The impact on a community for our four, five, and six day conventions was enormous. Therefore there was an incredible amount of preparations to be made. We had to discuss such logistics as how to transport the delegates from place to place, whom we should ask to speak and what they should talk about, and what we should do to entertain the wives. The conventions were large enough for us to attract some rather well-known actors and actresses, as well as senators and other well-known figures. Conventions were always a whole lot of fun.

I met some wonderful people during my time on the NSDA Board. One of them was Charley Millard, president of New York City Coca-Cola. His wife's name was Mary Anne. Pat Roddy, a bottler from Knoxville, Tennessee, and his wife Dottie were great friends. Pat's sister, Sis Mitchell, and her husband Jess remain very close friends. Anne and I see them at least once or twice a year. In addition, I remember meeting Charlie Broll, a Pepsi-Cola bottler, I believe, was from Wilmington, Delaware. He was an interesting character—a little younger than me. Imagine my amazement when, in talking to him, I found out that he had gone to Washington and Lee and had even belonged to the same fraternity as I did!

The gentleman who was president of the NSDA a few years before I came on board was Sid Mudd. Sid was a 7-Up bottler from New York City and was one of the most gentlemanly people I've probably ever known in my life. Sid was a fellow who led the NSDA fight. He was urbane, he was good looking, and he was smart. On a personal note, one of Sid's cousins— Roger Mudd, of television fame—was a fraternity brother and very good friend of mine in college. Historically speaking, both Sid and Roger were descendants of the famed Dr. Mudd, who treated the John Wilkes Booth when he was wounded after assassinating President Lincoln. But that's another story.

Along about this time, I was fortunate enough to be asked to serve on the Standardization Committee of the Coca-Cola Bottlers Association. This was an association begun in the early 1900's which protected individual bottlers from abuses by the Coca-Cola Company. It also allowed them to defend their franchise, defend their contracts, and maintain other standards deemed to be in the bottlers' interests.

The Coca-Cola Bottlers Association was located— as always—in Atlanta. As the years passed, it became involved in more and more facets of the industry, such as product liability insurance, automobile liability, worker compensation insurance, and many, many others. The association would buy insurance in great quantities, tailored to the needs of the bottling community, and then resell to the bottlers. My father was active for many years in the Coca-Cola Bottlers Association and served as its president from 1953 to 1954. In fact, when Dad retired from the board in the early 1960's, he was made only lifetime board member as far as I know. I have his plaque in my office; it was a gold plated card of which he was very proud.

The first person I ever knew to be involved in the CCBA was Ralph Beach, who was then the manager. Ralph and his wife, May, were great friends of my mother and father. When I was in California on duty in the Navy, they took me out to dinner. Ralph died some years ago and was succeeded by John Knox. John and his wife Laura became great friends of mine and Anne's.

During my time on CCBA Standardization Committee, we were in charge of such business as reviewing the uniforms, bottle standards, and all other manner of bottle standards except advertising. My cousin Mike served on the CCBA Board. The current president of the CCBA Board is Art Gregory. Art puts together great trips for the CCBA. Anne and I have been on several of them. They were great fun.

One of the other interesting bottling organizations I was asked to join was an outfit called Main Stream Bottlers. There was already an organization that the Coca-Cola Company had put together for New York, Atlanta, Chicago, New Orleans, and other communities that dealt with issues unique to larger cities. They would meet perhaps twice a year to listen to what the Coca-Cola Company had to say about their very specific problems. Main Stream Bottlers, in contrast, was designed with middle to smaller-sized bottlers in mind. Rome was included.

Homer Burrous, Vice-President of Marketing for Coca-Cola, was the fellow who came up with the concept of an organization for bottlers our size and who had similar problems. Rome was among the charter members. I believe that Bobby Wilkerson was the very first president. Bobby and I go back probably to 1957, when Bobby, whose father had been the manager of the Huntsville Coca-Cola bottling plant, went to work for the Thomas Company in Chattanooga, which was where Dalton bought its syrup. He and I instantly got along, and he remains to this day one of my favorite friends from the bottling industry. Bobby, however, is not an uncontroversial figure. He is a very aggressive sort of man who holds strong opinions. At the first indication that someone might be listening, Bobby will announce exactly what he thinks about anything and everything. He is a great individual.

Some other people who were friends of mine in those days include Neil Barry and John Tiernan. In fact, I still see John Tiernan to this day. I consider him to be an outstanding friend, and the two of us fish together occasionally.

The first meeting of the Main Stream Bottlers that I recall took place in 1976 or so in St. Maarten's, down in the West Indies. I remember the bottling community being greatly concerned that the Coca-Cola Company did not have a consistent attitude or plan. They kept changing things and seemed to have lost their vision.

At this point in time, Bryan Dyson first appeared on the scene. When he was first brought in out of South America, I considered him to be a very decisive sort of a fellow with his head on his shoulders. He understood marketing, and he understood the strengths of the bottling community. I would be remiss not to admit that Bryan could be rather rough around the edges. He did have something of a raucous mind, and he didn't hesitate to express his opinions in four letter words. But, as I've told Bryan on more than one occasion, he was the man who saved the Coca-Cola Company in those days. He helped everyone to understand that the Coca-Cola Company was not a science, but an art. He also brought to the business a real ability to distinguish the wheat from the chaff. If he thought the Coca-Cola Company's policies were wrong, he did not hesitate to take the side of the bottler. I can't praise Bryan Dyson enough for what he did for us.

The 1980s

In the 1980's, changes began to occur even faster than ever. The most significant of these changes was that we soon found ourselves losing control of the market. Kroger and several other supermarkets' desire for one representative from Coca-Cola to deal with several or even an entire region of stores made competition an interesting thing. Also, our competitors were forcing us into quite a few decisions that we did not like.

The demise of the returnable bottle was a huge factor that was coming more and more into play. As I've addressed earlier, one of the solutions to the Federal Trade Commission's ruling was based on the fact that returnable bottles constituted a major portion of the market. The thought, again previously stated, was that the bottles were ours. Were they to travel out of our territory, it would be a great economic loss to us.

By the 1980's, the returnable bottle was quickly becoming a thing of the past. Many times over the years, I've often heard consumers and environmentalists complaining to us for eliminating the returnable bottle and thus creating more pollution. But the fact is that the industry didn't do away with returnable bottles—it was the consumers themselves. The ten cents we required for a deposit on a bottle just wasn't enough to make people save them. They asked themselves if the inconvenience of saving their bottles and then taking them back to the store was worth ten cents, and the answer of course was "no."

To the bottlers, the economics of this situation was that bottles needed to be used somewhere in the order of twenty five to thirty five times in order for the bottler to come out ahead, because those bottles were terribly expensive. They were quality bottles, able to withstand the pressure of carbonation and the temperatures of the bottle washers. So along with the public's demand and the competitive nature of the industry came the can, the plastic bottle, and the NR (the non-returnable bottle). There just wasn't much anyone could do about it.

Another harbinger of major change was the growth of Pepsi-Cola into a formidable competitor. There were many regions where Pepsi outsold Coca-Cola by a fairly large margin, such as in South Carolina. The demands of the supermarkets, the demise of the returnable bottle, and the growth of Pepsi-Cola were all major factors in those days.

Somewhere around this time, Roberto Goizouta became Coca-Cola's heir apparent to the job of chairman of the Coca Cola Company . He and Don Keough were clearly becoming the leaders of the industry. It seems that Roberto was in charge of overseas growth and Don Keough took charge of domestic affairs. Don Keough, with his enormously attractive personality and infallible memory when it came to any aspect of bottling, was a strong champion for our business. Don's involvement in the public arena was enormously helpful to the industry.   For example, he became chairman of the Board of Trustees of Notre Dame, which reinforced the image of the Coca-Cola bottling community as "good folks." This was good public relations. Everyone agreed about Don's extraordinary good sense about the business. Bottlers genuinely loved the man. In my case, I still do.

Any discussion of the 1980's would be incomplete without referring to the merger mania of those days. Little by little, and then more and more, buyers began to ask, "What is your Coca-Cola plant worth, and would you be willing to sell it?" Of course, old Coca-Cola families such as ours said that we would never sell. There were some things that were sacred in those days, and an old family-run business was one of them.

The 1980's were also the era of "the new taste of Coca-Cola." Wow, what a blast that was! A Pepsi-Cola bottler in Dallas, Texas developed a marketing tool known as "The Pepsi Challenge." What he did was to set two cups of soft drinks in front of a consumer. One was marked "Cup A" and one was marked "Cup B." Hidden behind so that the person tasting couldn't see, were a Coca-Cola bottle and a Pepsi bottle.

What this fellow in Texas would do was to go into malls and ask people which drink they liked better. They usually picked Pepsi, and so Pepsi began to beat our socks off. It seems that Pepsi just tasted better to the consumer. The facts were that it had to do with the sweetness. Pepsi was sweeter, and at first taste it did taste better. The Coca-Cola Company panicked. We knew that something just had to be done. Could it be that the taste of Coke was really not as good as the taste of Pepsi? What a horrible thought to entertain! It was part of the conversation in the hallowed halls of North Avenue (as the headquarters was known as because it was located on North Avenue in Atlanta). So along came a project called "Project Kansas." (We bottlers were not aware of many of these happenings until much later.)

The new taste tests were collected and analyzed by Dr. Roy Stout, Coca-Cola's mathematical statistician. Anyway, Roy simply insisted that the right thing for us to do was to reformulate the taste of Coke. Very suddenly, the announcement came that Coca-Cola Company, based on Roy's data, had decided to reformulate Coca-Cola. An extravagant party was thrown to announce the change. Here's how it happened:

One day in April of 1985, we were asked to go to the High Museum in Atlanta for a big meeting. Roberto and the others put on a great dog and pony show about how the new taste had been tested over and over again and how the right thing to do was to change from the old flavor to the new one. I had been invited by the company to be a representative bottler—that is, to fly early the next morning to New York City where I would be entertained, along with more bottlers, at the 21 Club. Then, we were to attend a press conference in Kennedy Center as guests of Roberto Goizueta in a huge auditorium at the Kennedy Center. It was to be a big show put on in front of national television, breaking into the newscasts. The one hundred year-old Coca-Cola formula was going to be changed. Well, it was an occasion to be thrilled about. That night at 21 Club, everybody stood up and gave a little speech. I even offered a few comments myself—something to the tune of if my grandfather were still living and if he thought this was the right move to make, he would say "right on." I certainly concurred with that.

However, the next day at the press conference, Roberto was challenged by some of the reporters. It soon became apparent that he was uncomfortable with some of the answers he gave. (Of course, I say all of this in retrospect. At the time, I was in no way opposed to this move nor did I fear it.)

At first, I thought that the new formula was going to be the greatest thing in the world. Part of the reason behind my excitement goes back to the fact that basically, in the Coca-Cola business, route salesmen didn't have much talk about out in the stores. What do you say about Coca-Cola to a person who has grown up in the state of Georgia that he or she doesn't already know? Well, when the new taste of Coke came along, boy did we have something to talk about! Everybody wanted to talk to Coca-Cola salesmen. "Why did you change?" they asked. "What does it taste like?"

Earlier, I pointed out that the reason Pepsi-Cola was selected over Coca-Cola in the taste tests was that it tasted sweeter. This was true. What Roy Stout's research and our thinking didn't do was to finish that research. The truth was that the first two or three sips were good, but after that the Pepsi-Cola became too sweet for many consumers. Had the taste tests insisted that a person drink an entire cup of the product, by the time that person had finished half of the cup, he or she would probably desire to switch to Coca-Cola. However, we didn't have this information at the time. We panicked as an industry and thought that sweeter meant better. That didn't turn out to be that case.

It didn't take long for most bottlers to realize that we had a real problem on our hands. As the new formula went out into the stores, the complaints started rolling in. Things got so bad in Rome that Anne was getting phone calls at our home during the day and even at night. She would answer the phone, and people would scream obscenities, yelling "What did you do to my Coke?" and hanging up. People would call me in the office, mad as devil, saying "You ruined our Coke!" "You took it away from us!" Caller after caller threatened to change over to Pepsi. It was a real bad scene.

Anne and I were scheduled to go on a cruise to Alaska in June, but I was very hesitant to take the trip. I was worried I would miss too much of the events that were transpiring. Then I thought to myself, "Why not? I need to get away from all of this mess. It's the worst thing that could have ever happened." So we went on our cruise. We made many friends on the trip.

As we were disembarking from the ship, and as I said we had made many friends, Anne and I ended up in front of the line for customs and passport control. The lady in charge of passports was asking me questions. Never looking up, she asked, "Mr. Barron, you live in Rome, GA?" And I replied, "Yes, ma'am." She asked what I did for a living and I said "I'm a Coca-Cola bottler." Then she looked up at me with fire in her eyes and said, "What did you do to my Coca-Cola?" I said that I hadn't done anything. With that, she shouted, pointed her pencil at me and told me to get out of there. It was very embarrassing. I began to look up and down the line at all the friends that I had met on the ship. They were all looking at me like I was a Communist.

Life went on. I do remember going to the Coca-Cola Company for lunch one day at the height of the New Coke mess. Roy Stout was sitting at the table in the executive dining room, and I went to him and asked, "Roy, are you sure about all of this?" He assured me that his data still hadn't changed and that we were still on the right track. However, I still felt that something was not quite right. We were about ten weeks into the campaign, but there was still such horrible harassing of the Coca-Cola Company. Consumers were calling in every day and saying we had made a terrible mistake. The New Coke formula had been the wrong thing to do.

Finally, one day I got a phone call from Earl Leonard. He said to me, "Frank, we've had enough. We're going to capitulate." I told him I was delighted to hear the news. I added, however, that our announcement should be humble in every respect. The company had made a mistake, and everyone knew it.

Earl read me the release that was going to be announced by Don Keough. It was indeed a very humble statement. One part of that speech that I know I will never forget was Don's great reply as to whether we had changed the formula to stimulate conversation or if it had been a public relations move. Don said, "We're not that dumb, and we're not that smart. We changed to formula because we thought we were right, but clearly we were wrong. You said, 'Bring back our old Coke.' Here it is."

When we started to bring our old syrup back, consumers were so hungry for their old Coca-Colas that we were bottling syrup that had been manufactured that morning. Of course, there is an aging process in any kind of food production, and people in our community were accustomed to drinking Cokes with syrup that was at least eight days old. When the old formula Coca-Colas hit the streets again, people were sucking them up with the syrup being only about three days old. Nothing was wrong with it, nothing better or worse, but it just tasted different because of the time involved.

There was, however, a small reaction from consumers because of the different taste the aging created. We worried, "Oh no—now we've really messed things up!" But in actuality, business picked up at an incredible pace. Customers were walking into stores and demanding, "I want my old Coca-Cola. I want to see if it's as good as I remember." Our business for the next three or four months was probably better than it had ever been. It was probably the most unusual marketing phenomena ever to happen in The United States.

Economists and marketing consultants began expressing their amazement over the entire incident. The president of Pepsi-Cola Company wrote a book entitled The Other Guy Blinked. There were a couple of books written by the folks down in Atlanta, and a man named Taylor wrote a book about what had happened with Project Kansas. Tom Oliver wrote a book about the New Taste of Coke and how it came about, and the Coca-Cola Company let him in to interview many people. He even interviewed me and quoted me in the book. He talked to Keough and everyone else. That entire event was such a strange phenomenon. No one was happier than me when it was all over with.

The Decision to Sell

As a result of the New Coke situation, we got the feeling in our own halls that the Coca-Cola industry as a whole was headed for some real problems. We were already feeling the pressures toward consolidation, and another issue was the fact that we had so little local control over advertising. Television schedules had to be made centrally because our advertisers couldn't wait for fifty of so bottlers to get together and agree on ad campaigns. The amount of money required to fund these advertisements was phenomenal.

Individual bottlers were losing more and more control over their own destiny. Many of us began to wonder about what we should do. There was the technical side of the business that had grown by leaps and bounds, and fast bottling equipment was becoming very available. So the heads of the Coca-Cola Company made a decision. They said they would issue contracts to small Coca-Cola plants so that instead of being regular bottlers, the smaller plants would change over to being "marketing bottlers". This meant that the bigger plants would start bottling for the little guys, who in turn would market and not be required to bottle.

Under the new marketing bottler concept, the perpetual contracts would be null and void. A new contract would be issued, which was substantially the same as the old perpetual one. But there were a couple of other little clauses that the Coca-Cola Company wanted to add to our new contracts, such as granting the Coca-Cola Company the right to modify the price of syrup as they saw fit and the right of first refusal if we wanted to sell our franchise. Some bottlers went ahead and became marketing bottlers, others decided to tough it out and do the best they could.

The decision to allow the Coca-Cola Company to control the price of syrup was instigated by the Freeman brothers in New Orleans. Dick and Louis Freeman were extremely good bottlers, and they viewed the pricing structure that was in effect in those days as being archaic. It was based on, as I recall, about $1.40 per gallon plus the price of sugar. They thought that the Coca-Cola Company needed more money for television, marketing, and promotion, and they were right. Many of us agreed and became some of the first, as we termed it in those days, "amending bottlers." That is, we amended our contract so that the Coca-Cola Company could raise the price of syrup within set guidelines. Those guidelines had to do with raising the price upon three month notification and justification of advertising expenses.

It became increasingly clear that there were strains between the Coca-Cola Company and the bottlers that were not going to go away. And according to our perspective, the situation was only going to worsen. Inevitably we found ourselves asking the big question: "Should we sell?"

Sometime in the early 1980's, as a board member of the NSDA, I was very much involved in these and all sorts of other questions that were being asked by bottlers everywhere. Mike was a member of the board of the Coca-Cola Bottlers Association and was hearing more of the bottler's side of issues. I found myself more involved in industry affairs.

I don't mean to imply by any stretch of the imagination that the Coca-Cola Bottlers Association was anti-Coca-Cola Company—they weren't. We all recognized that if anything happened to the Coca-Cola Company that we would all go down the tube. Some bottlers viewed it as a "We versus they" situation, but the thinking bottlers didn't. However, we could all clearly see that strife was headed our way.

Our dealings with the Federal Trade Commission, the ban on saccharine, the challenges to the exclusivity of the franchises, and many other difficulties the industry faced soon began to take their toll. Towards the beginning of the 1980's, we noted a general sense of discontent among the bottlers. There was no joy throughout the land of Coca-Cola. There was bitterness in our meetings, Pepsi-Cola was on a roll, and Royal Crown was beginning to make headlines. It looked as if Coca-Cola was being transformed into just an everyday, generic sort of brand. Those of us who were friends with Luke Smith and Jim Wimberly in Atlanta were constantly talking with them about these problems.

Alfred, Mike, Al, and I were the delegates from Rome to carry our arguments to Atlanta. The major trouble was that we saw that our exclusive franchise was beginning to lose value. Miami Coca-Cola had been sold, as had Atlanta. So we sat down and sharply analyzed what our options were. Initially Mike, Al, and I decided that the best strategy was for us to expand. We were young, we were aggressive, and we liked what we were doing. In regards to transportation, with our airplane we were as mobile as we could be. We periodically make trips down to Brunswick or Waycross attempting to acquire their plants, but these trips were largely unsuccessful. Some people still did not want to sell out. Then, one day in 1983, we were invited to consider purchasing the Coca-Cola plant in Tallahassee, Florida. Our deliberations with Tallahassee provided an interesting situation that bears some discussion.

The Tallahassee plant was owned by a family whose name I don't recall. However, I do remember that it was brokered by a fellow named George Overend. George and I had been friends for quite some time—at least since the mid 1960's. One day, George called me and informed me that he was involved in negotiations to sell Tallahassee Coca-Cola. He knew that we could easily access the area because of our plant down in Valdosta.

Four entities were invited to bid on Tallahassee. They were Rome Coca-Cola, Jack Lupton's plants (which essentially covered the state of Florida as well as Dallas, Denver and other cities), the Crawford Rainwater group out of Pensacola, and the Crawford Johnson group out of Birmingham. We went down to look at the territory, and we saw many problems. However, we thought we saw many different economies we could affect. We predicted that with Valdosta we could leverage the deal. The Tallahassee plant's annual production was about 700,000 cases.

Representatives from the four different entities were invited to submit sealed bids. The minimum bid had to be $3.5 million, and the winning bid had to be $250,000 higher than the second bid. If it wasn't, the top two bidders would sit down ten days later for an open bidding process, face to face.

Alfred Lee, Mike, Al, and I sat down and did some arithmetic. At first, we thought that $3.5 million was a rather high starting point. We didn't see how we could pay for that in the first place, but we wanted to play the game. (We had paid $1,010,000 for Valdosta some 17 or 18 years previously and were still struggling to pay back our debts there. We could well imagine what paying back $3.5 million would be like.) But before jumping in, we did some more analysis. We predicted that if $3.5 million was the minimum bid, in order to win the plant we would have to bid $3.75 million to get the $250,000 spread. Then we thought that someone would bid a slight bit above the $3.75 million to make certain they had the spread. So, we assumed that it would take right at 4 million and one dollars to buy Tallahassee.

We began to think about how we would go about acquiring $4 million dollars. First of all, we knew we couldn't go back and ask the rest of the Rome stockholders—that being my mother, the Kathleen Barron Brennan Estate; Alfred Lee, who was in his late sixties and really didn't want to acquire any more debt; and my sister, who was not interested. (Perhaps I should mention at this point that a few years previously my sister had opted out of Valdosta.

George Overend brokered a deal in which she sold her quarter to us for $750,000.) So, we couldn't use Rome as leverage, and we just couldn't imagine how our $1 million Valdosta plant could bear a $4 million acquisition. Somewhat sorrowfully, we asked Tallahassee to let us out of the bid. We just didn't think we could finance the acquisition.

As it turned out, our predictions turned out to be exactly on the mark. 4 million and one dollars would have bought the plant. The top bid was somewhere around $3.75 million. Clearly as it happened, the two plants that bid on Tallahassee were closer together than the $250,000 minimum. The open bidding process did take place. Ten days after the original bid, the plant had sold for something in the excess of $6 million dollars.

With the high prices that we saw bottlers willing to pay for cases of Coca-Cola, I think those of us in Rome began to wonder if we were in the right business anymore. After we saw what was paid for Tallahassee, we saw was an industry that would inevitably kill itself. Perhaps we misread the situation, but what we came to understand was that there were two types of bottlers in the business—the buyers and the sellers. The question was, which one were we?

I must add that by this time, the Coca-Cola Company's leadership had turned 180 degrees. Roberto Goizueta was in the saddle and actively moving. Don Keough was the president of Coca-Cola USA, and Roberto was chairman of the board. They made just a wonderful team; things were looking good. The Coca-Cola Company sold several of the little satellite operations that it had acquired over the years: a shrimp farm, a wine business, and a large venture in the movie business. The company decided that it was, in essence, a soft drink company. This contrasted with the fact that Pepsi-Cola had become very involved in the food business with Lay's Potato Chips, Kentucky Fried Chicken, Pizza Hut, and a few others.

It soon became apparent to us that as much as we wanted to remain a part of the company, our days as bottlers were numbered. We mulled this over individually. I'm not sure that there was a time prior to December of 1985 when we all sat down to discuss the situation, but when we did we all agreed that we should think about getting out of the business. Also, we each began to look at our individual family situations. As I mentioned earlier, there were three families involved in the business. There was the Willie Barron family, consisting of Virginia and myself; the Alfred Lee family, consisting of Alfred and his two boys; and the Kathleen Brennan family. Considering everyone in the extended family, there were three men: Mike, Al, and me. Mike and Al represented Alfred Lee, I represented myself and Virginia, and no one represented Kathleen. We began to see that it was a bit unfair for Mike, Al, Alfred Lee, and me to always be the ones to go on conventions and buy new cars. Also, the three of us were paid large salaries because we had sacrificed dividends to make the business grow stronger. We could tell that there were going to be pressures from the other sides to pay more dividends or have more perks. Mike, Al, and I basically did not own the business. We perhaps owned half of it, but we didn't own it all.

We realized that the business was, in all practicality, unable to grow any larger and that our size was limited. Our multiples were entirely too high, and our outside stockholders would never go along with us to help leverage the business. In addition, we found ourselves limited geographically. We toyed around with the idea of acquiring Ellijay, Jasper, and some other small communities. I even spoke to Bryan Dyson at the Coca-Cola Company about the deal, but he was totally uninterested. We were limited in being able to move north because the Birmingham folks owned a great portion of the territory up in Tennessee. Similarly, we couldn't move west because that area was owned by the Crawford Rainwater group in

Florida, and they were clearly on an aggressive move to expand. South of us was Atlanta, which wasn't available. We found ourselves rather fenced in.

As time passed, Alfred Lee, Mike, Al, and I began having the same type of thought in the fall of 1985. We said to each other, "You know, it's been a great run, but maybe it's time we began thinking about something else." So we sat down and considered our numbers. We were producing somewhere around 6 million cases at that time. Multiplied at $10 a case, the figure came out to be somewhere around $60 million. Then the question became, "Should we take the $60 million and, as a family, invest it in treasury bonds, or should we just sit still?" The more we thought about this question, the more we realized that for us, the wise thing to do was to sell out. Gingerly at first, and then with more confidence as the weeks went by, we began talking among ourselves more and more. Finally, one day in December we realized that the time had come to talk to a lawyer so we could inquire about our options.

By this time, Jack Lupton had already announced that he was going to sell. (Jack Lupton's operations covered about ten percent of the population of the United States.) Beatress Food had announced that it was going to sell, and their territories constituted another ten percent. We didn't know it then, but the Freeman boys in New Orleans had decided that they were going to sell as well.

As we saw these events transpiring, we decided to call George Overend. I will never forget it. We met George for lunch on December 24 at the Holiday Inn Skytop and said, "George, what do you think?" We had quite a lengthy discussion. George told us that given the facts that we were close to Atlanta and that we were among the highest per capita groups around, and also considering our reputation and the state of our market, we could probably command the highest price that had ever been paid for an organization of

Coca-Cola plants. We discussed the numbers. The numbers sounded good.

After the day's discussion, we told George that he was on retainer while we started planning a strategy. Then, shortly after the first of the year, we had George approach the Coca-Cola Company with a fairly extensive document which named our price. The price was in excess of $84 million. Of course this was split between 12 families in varying percentages. This also included the Lettie Pate Evans Foundation which owned part of the plants. (The price became a matter of public knowledge later, when the CCE was formed and the price Coca-Cola had paid for us was openly documented.) It worked out to around $12.50 per case, which was more or less unheard of in those days. The reason I am able to recall so precisely the amount for which we sold our plant is because the original CCE prospectus listed not only what the organization paid for our business, but also how much we had earned for the previous two or three years. So we were pretty much open for the world to see. As George Overend likes to say, "We opened our kimono, and there we were!"

The deal to the Coca-Cola Company was that they had two weeks to consider the matter and to give us an answer one way or another. If Coca-Cola declined, the agreement was that we would feel free to look for a buyer anywhere in the world. About ten days later, the Coca-Cola Company agreed to buy.

Right in the middle of these dramatic days for us, I had to go to Atlanta in my capacity as a Board Member of Berry School to meet with the Woodruff Foundation. Jimmy Sibley and Bill Bowdon, also on the Berry Board were to attend the meeting as well. We were to meet with Ivan Allen and Don Keough to express our gratitude for the way the Woodruff Foundation had treated Berry College. I told Alfred Lee that I was going to be having lunch with Don Keough and I thought the time had come to mention our plans to him. So before I left, we planned that at

10:00, as I was leaving Rome, Alfred would call Keough and inform him of our decision to sell out. If Don had a few minutes after lunch, I would sit down and fill him in on the details.

As soon as I arrived at the Coca-Cola Company, we all went up to the dining room where everyone was waiting. Don and I cast a couple of glances at each other. John White, who was Don's executive assistant, approached me and said, "Frank, if you and Don could talk for a few minutes after lunch, he would be very grateful." I replied that I would love to as long as Don was certain he could spare the time. So we went through the lunch and dealt with the Berry business, and then I went to speak with Don.

I walked into his office and sat down. It was just the two of us. Suddenly, Don picked up a pencil and broke it, clearly upset. He said, "This is not what I wanted to happen!" He said that Coca-Cola did not want to own its own bottlers. I told Don that I agreed with him on everything except that last statement. In my opinion, Coca-Cola should own its own bottlers. There was no reason in the world why the company shouldn't be able to tell bottlers to take on Minute Maid, for example, or to participate in a particular television campaign. It just couldn't tell bottlers such things with one arm tied behind its back. Don said, "Yes, the company could work that way, just let me tell you how it would work." He said that Coca-Cola could simply tell its bottlers that certain decisions were in the company's best interest, and the bottlers should follow along. I replied that I was a stockholder in the Coca-Cola Company as well as being a bottler, and I was just offering my opinions. (As I mentioned earlier, Don and I go back to the 1960's when we first met at the Harvard Business School, and so we were very close to each other.)

At this point, Don offered to tell me what he termed "the story of the new company." He said that Jack Lupton had called him up before Christmas, on a Monday, and told him he would like to have dinner with Don the following Wednesday. Don agreed. Jack told Don, "There are 147 Luptons that are dependent on this company for their livelihood, but not a single one of them cares anything about running the business. When I'm gone, the company is going to be headless, and I think too much of the business to let that happen." Jack Lupton offered to sell out to Don.

Of course, that's the way things should have been. Don said that on Friday they had announced the formation of the new Coca-Cola Enterprises (CCE). They didn't know what it was going to be or how it was going to be financed, so they had no knowledge of what to do. But that's how it started. Of course, subsequently, we sold our business to the Coca-Cola Company, and soon afterwards the Freemans sold to the Coca-Cola Company as well. Later on, CCE was formed to buy those bottlers from the Coca-Cola Company.

After I left Don's office and went back to Rome that day, events transpired rather rapidly. The sale closed in late July, and July 31 was our last day. But there were several events that occurred between our agreement to sell and the closing day. Between January of 1986, when we had first agreed to sell, and the time that we closed the deal, we went through a process known then as "Due Diligence." Jim Ford, an auditor and researcher for the Coca-Cola Company, was the person who corresponded with our CPA's. The marketing division came in and surveyed. We had to prepare lists of our trucks and coolers. Other items we had to catalogue included the furniture and even the pictures that hung in my office! (There were many Coca-Cola artifacts and things of that nature. I have a letter listing them that gave them to me.)

We contacted all of the stockholders that were involved. Clarence Archer was a participant in Dalton, and the Lettie Pate Evans family in Atlanta was a very small participant in the Fort Valley operation. Those situations were really very simple because they were a part of the overall scheme of things. We used

Southland, Asbell, and Brennen as our law firm. Mike Egan, of course, was very involved in the entire affair. There were so many things for us to do!

One of the most difficult parts of the whole situation was explaining to our employees and longtime associates the reason why we were selling. We kept our decision a secret for many months, but sometime in April we finally decided to make the announcement. Rumors had already been floating through the community. There had been too many leaks in Atlanta and in Rome, and soon we found ourselves the subject of newspaper headlines. We were subjected to too many questions, interviews, and the whole bit. It was not an easy time. But the Coca-Cola Company was as helpful to us as they could be, offering to let us use their facilities whenever we had need of them.

For me personally, one of the most difficult situations occurred during a visit to Atlanta. I called Earl Leonard and asked if he had a few minutes for me to stop by and visit with him. He replied that he was rather busy and requested that we meet at a later date. I thought it would be best that Earl hear the news from me than from an outside source, so I told Earl then and there that we were selling our business. Whatever it was that Earl had to do, he dropped it. I went by and spoke for quite a while with Earl, explaining to him about the Brennan family (which at that time Earl didn't even know existed). I think that some of the dramatic changes that the bottling community was undergoing came as quite a surprise to him.

Before we closed in July and the money was actually wired to our bank, several other Coca-Cola plants decided to sell as well. In fact, between 1985 and 1990, I would estimate that 60 percent of the Coca-Cola population of the United States had either sold to CCE or was in some way controlled by the Coca-Cola Company. The entire Coca-Cola business changed in a very short period of time. I think that selling a business that has been in a family as long as ours had is one of the most traumatic experiences a man can go through. My grandfather had started out in January of 1901, and here we were 85 years later selling our heritage.

One day, as we were getting very close to the closing day, I was in my office in Rome. We were just about at the end of the conversation in Alfred Lee's office and all that remained to be done was the final cutting of the money. In the middle of the meeting, I was summoned out of the office to an urgent phone call. It was Richard Hiller.

Richard was Senior Vice-President of Coca-Cola, and he said that he wanted to offer me a job. He said that he wanted for me to stay on with the company in any way that I would like. His offer, of course, was very flattering to me, but the truth of the matter was that I was getting tired. I was 55 or 56 at the time. I had been getting up at 5:15 every morning and staying at work until 6:00 or 6:30 every night for 30 years. Some of the fun had gone out of the business, and I had pretty much done everything that I had wanted to do. Richard replied that I could work to any degree that I liked and that I could keep my office and a part-time secretary. So, I agreed to stay on. It was originally a three-year contract, a sum which I thought was very good compensation. I remember saying to Richard that I wanted the record to show that our conversation had taken place after the signing of the agreement to sell. He said that was the very reason why he had waited until this day to call me.

I stayed on with the company until after the July 31 closing. I would go down to the office around 8:00 in the morning, read the newspaper, clear out my desk some more, answer the telephone, and deal with people's questions. In actuality, there was an avalanche of questions about the new team that had come in. (Of course, Alfred, Mike, and Al had moved out.) I suppose that in many ways that was the best way of making the transition for them.

It became apparent to me after six or eight weeks, however, that I simply couldn't stay. The employees would come to me and exclaim, "Frank, you're never going to believe what they're doing!" It was very difficult for me to explain to them that the business wasn't ours anymore. Soon, I found out from Alfred, Mike, and Al that there was room for me in their new office downtown. Alfred, Mike, and Al went in a different direction, and subsequently I did too

I was promised 25 percent of Karen Stinson's time for the writing of my personal letters, which they were very gracious to offer. But my 25 percent kept getting smaller and smaller. The situation just wasn't working out. Karen came to work for the Coca-Cola Company in 1978. She was soon assigned to me to do my bookkeeping for Cartersville and Dalton. More and more of her time was taken up by my dictation and bookkeeping so it was only natural that she worked full time for me. I called Karen and told her I was moving out and asked her if she would be remotely interested in going with me. She responded, "When is our last day?" I said, "Right now," and so she turned in her notice. She still works for me and has worked with me over half of her life. She and her husband have raised two fine children. She is very good and her greatest asset is she knows all of my friends and besides which she refuses to take any abnormal abuse from me and thus keeps me in line. I don't know how I could get along without her.

The arrangement with the Coca-Cola Company didn't work out as well as I had planned. I soon moved downtown. Shortly thereafter I bought the old Rhodes Furniture Store building which I renovated into offices and a retail space for rental.

That's about the end of this story. The Coca-Cola Company moved on the make several changes that we would not have had the heart to make, such as eliminating helpers and cutting back on customer service. I'm really rather glad that we didn't have to be involved with that. We took our money and ran. In retrospect, I don't regret our decision. There are days when I am nostalgic for what used to be—the old days, the camaraderie, the people. Perhaps I had gotten older or perhaps I had gotten jaded, but for whatever reason, I have never looked back. So ends the saga of the Rome Coca-Cola Associated Plants.

My Service in the Navy

My official Navy discharge rank was William F. Barron, Jr. 565841/1105 LT(JG) USNR. I served on board the USS EVERSOLE (DD-789) from January 1953 to December 1955. During that time, I served in several capacities: Electrical Engineer, Damage Control Assistant, and finally, as Chief Engineer.

As previously stated, I was born in Rome, Georgia on December 31, 1931. Except for my time in the U.S. Navy or in school, I have lived in the Rome community all of my life. I attended Darlington Schools, and in 1952 I earned a degree in business administration at Washington & Lee University in Lexington, Virginia.

In September 1952, I entered Officers Candidate School (OCS Class VIII) and was commissioned on December 21 of that same year. After a short leave, I went to San Francisco where I boarded the MSTS GENERAL W.A. MANN. From there it was a two-week trip to Yokosuka, Japan, where I reported to a Gearing (DD-692) class destroyer, the USS EVERSOLE . We then proceeded to duty on what was known as "the bomb line."

The bomb line duty involved harassing and interdiction fire north of the 38th parallel off the coast of Korea. It also included the screening of aircraft carriers, which consisted partially of screening for submarines and partially of screening for plane guard activities that were stationed behind the aircraft carriers.

Displacing about 2,250 tons of water and measuring 390 by 40 feet, the USS EVERSOLE was a mighty ship. It was powered by four Babcock-Wilcox A-frame boilers, which in turn powered two Westinghouse steam turbine engines. The ship was armed with three twin five-inch 38 millimeter guns and two three-inch 50 millimeter guns, in addition to the five torpedo tubes amidships on the 01 Deck. We were allowed to house 21 officers and 290 enlisted men. However, to have such a high number of enlisted men was very, very unusual. We managed to keep our officer complement, but at times we would find ourselves low on enlisted men.

The USS EVERSOLE was, in fact, the second ship named after Lt. John T. Eversole. (The first EVERSOLE had been sunk during the latter part of WWII.) An Annapolis graduate, Lt. Eversole was a torpedo bomber who had been killed at the battle of Midway. He had served in TBS 61 on board USS ENTERPRISE (CV-6). Although I don't know much else about him, I do know from the picture hanging in the wardroom that he had been a lean, handsome fellow with black hair.

My first General Quarters station was in Plot, where the Mark I Able computer (a mechanical computer of that era) was located. This computer aimed the guns during fire missions in Korea. My job at GQ was to add a hundred yards or so to the right or left, depending on the requests of the shore fire control spotter. The process was done by off-set firing. We were asked to fire on certain grid coordinates, then we would then be asked to correct the fire in small increments. When the aim was correct, we would "fire for effect." At that point, we would turn loose of all our firepower.

One of the most interesting things that I did during the Korean War was to do some shore spotting. It was decided that the Marines, who were the shore spotters, and the Navy, who was launching fire from sea, should exchange duties for a brief time so that each could experience exactly what was happening on the other side. This meant that I was assigned to go ashore to the hills of Korea for several days. I was supposed to perform some of the shore spotting, but we never got around to it.

I was sent over in the captain's gig to a place called "Silver Beach." A Marine encampment was located there. Two or three of the Marine lieutenants took me under their wing, and away we went into the mountains. We would get up early every morning and ride a Jeep back through several passes. We would climb hills, get into the trenches, and look north across the Korean mountains. Because it was April or perhaps even May, there was not much snow left on the ground. I could very clearly see that there were strange white specks all over the hills. When I asked what they were, I was told that the white specks were the bodies of dead North Koreans that had been killed during the previous winter. They stood out on the hill because their camouflage had been white. Apparently the North Koreans did not have the same ethic about removing their wounded and dead as we did. The bodies were just left where they had fallen.

As we were standing in one of the trenches there on the hill, one of the two lieutenants remarked to the other, "You know, I think that place where Barron is standing is the exact same spot where a fellow got hit by a sniper the other day." Of course, you can imagine my shock! I hit the bottom of that trench as quickly as I could. They all laughed, and I realized I was being teased. All in all, that was quite an experience.

One interesting thing about this particular trip is that we had a Catholic chaplain on board our ship. He was a Lieutenant named Donald Rooney. I've never known what happened to him, but he was a great fellow. Earlier in his career, Donald had met a Korean chaplain whom he knew to live near Silver Beach (very close to where we were stationed). Donald had accompanied us on the shore spotting trip, and so one night I went with him to visit his friend. There I was in a Korean hut (which is a small, dirt house), with a bunch of Korean children, their families, and two Catholic chaplains, one American and one Korean. It was a fascinating evening that I have never forgotten. Many years later, while in conversation with Roy Stout, who you may recall was the Officer with The Coca-Cola Company in charge of statistical data that indicated the new taste of Coke was the right thing to do. Roy and I in a conversation discovered that we had both been at Silver Beach at the same time. He was a Navy Officer who was permanently stationed there. I'm sure we met because there weren't but five or six officers there at the time. Neither one of us remember each other though.

When we arrived home from Korea in mid-1953, I was sent to The Damage Control School at Treasure Island in San Francisco. Afterwards, I went to the Engineering Department afterwards, whereupon my GQ station was changed to Damage Control (located at midship). For my final year at the General Quarters station, I was stationed in the forward engine room, where I served as Chief Engineer.

For my first year on board the ship, I stood Junior Officer of the Deck watches on the bridge, after which time I was qualified as an Officer of the Deck Underway. I stood OOD Watches Underway during the second year. Then, during my third year, a Chief Engineer on another ship allowed a boiler to ignite and burn up in flames. His defense was that he was standing OOD watches and thus could not look after the boiler. Immediately, Commander Cruisers and Destroyers Pacific (COMCRUDESPAC) issued an order prohibiting Chief Engineers from standing OOD Watches Underway, except in extreme emergencies. Needless to say, I did not stand any more OOD Watches during my last year.

The best way to describe my time in the Navy is to tell a series of stories and incidents that perhaps offer something of the flavor of my service.

As a new officer on board (and a USNR OCS fellow at that), I knew nothing. The first person I met was a fellow named LT (JG) Robinson, an Annapolis graduate. I insisted on calling him "Sir" or "Mr. Robinson" the first two or three weeks. One day he looked around and said, "Mr. Barron, are you by any chance related to Blue Barron, the orchestra leader?"

"No sir, Mr. Robinson," I replied.

"Well, as far as I'm concerned," he said, "from here on out you are 'Blue Barron'."

He then asked me to call him "Ace" instead of "Mr. Robinson." Actually, he was only about a year older than I was, so it seemed natural for me to call him "Ace." From that time on, things were much more relaxed between the two of us.

My first skipper was CDR Victor Delano (CAPT. USN. RET.). Victor, now retired, remains one of the best friends I have ever had. He was an outstanding naval officer who served on the USS WEST VIRGINIA, which was one of the battleships located on Battleship Row in Pearl Harbor. I have a copy of the story of his escape from the ship during the Japanese attack at Pearl Harbor, which he penned for his father. His account of climbing up a small escape hatch and performing other such feats in order to escape from the bowels of that ship is a truly extraordinary one. I have always considered Victor to be a wonderful person—a true gentleman of the first order. I see him as often as possible.

In early February of 1953, soon after I reported onboard, we were instructed to go directly from Hong Kong to Guam, where we were to escort a Navy freighter from Guam to Yokosuka (the Navy port in Tokyo.) We proceeded directly to Guam, where we spent the night in preparation for leaving early the next morning.

One of the interesting incidents that happened on that night related to my roommate, who was a North Korean Ensign by the name of In Su Chung. In Su was a wonderful fellow—a musician by trade who had been commissioned in the South Korean Navy. He was sent onboard the EVERSOLE to serve as an interpreter and to learn how to operate destroyers. When we got off the ship that night in Guam, we were all going over to the officers' club. However, the officer of the day refused to let In Su off the ship because he was not a U.S. citizen. We had quite a row with this officer and were told if we could have our request approved by the duty command officer, then In Su could go. We did so, and in the process we disturbed a Lieutenant Commander from playing bridge, as I recall. He came out, looked at us, and looked at Chung. Then he said, "Well, In Su can go with you, but if anything happens, Barron, it's your tail."

The next morning, we left running about a mile and a half or two miles ahead of the Navy freighter, protecting it from enemy submarines or any other misfortunate encounters. After about a day or so, we were told by light signals—rather urgently in fact—that we were to take station forty miles ahead. The captain, having never been told to maintain such an incredible distance between his ship and his charge, questioned the orders for clarification. He was told that the orders were indeed correct.

Can you believe they let these children run a ship?

Of course, we immediately complied with orders and soon found ourselves in Yokosuka several days later. Captain Delano went down to the officers' club when we arrived, and he happened to run into the skipper of the Navy freighter—a fellow that he had known before. Delano asked the skipper if he could explain the strange orders we had received. Since Delano was cleared for secret and had the need to know, the skipper informed him that our ship had in reality been escorting an atomic bomb.

History tells us that in those days, the newly-elected President of the United States, Dwight Eisenhower had threatened the North Koreans and the Chinese with an atomic bomb if they did not proceed immediately with signing a truce and settling the exchange of prisoners. I suppose it was our ship that escorted that very bomb. The reason we had been told to take station forty miles ahead was that there had been a fire on the freighter. The commanding officer decided if the freighter were to explode, our ship just might survive the blast if we were forty miles out in front. Of course, I never knew any of this information until recent years in conversations with Captain Delano. The story has provided me with several interesting thoughts.

But back to my service in Korea. My first experience with enemy fire came in early April 1953, when we were posted inside Wonsan Harbor. We were running patrols to protect the spotter islands located inside that harbor. On these islands, air control personnel directed our airplanes in and out of missions in North Korea then back up. Very clear directions were given to us concerning which parts of the harbor had been swept by the minesweepers and which parts were known to be dangerous.

The area we were patrolling was called "Cigarette." It was about four miles long and one mile wide. We would travel up and down the area, making figure eights, ovals, and circles. As long as we stayed inside the cleared area, we were safe. But the North Koreans soon began to pick certain spots inside Cigarette and train a number of guns on them—mostly 155mm. They assumed that at some point we would go through the area they had targeted, and they would then be able to blast us out of the water. The theory seemed very logical, and we all feared finding that spot.

One day I was on the bridge standing a JOOD Watch. It was sunny day in April, but there was still snow on the mountains. The scene was absolutely beautiful. I recall standing there when suddenly the ship was bracketed by splashes. I thought, "O Lord! This is it! We'll soon be hit, and then we will sink." My next thought was, "If my Mama knew what you fellows are trying to do, you wouldn't do it then!" I laughed about that quite frequently in later years.

That day was my first baptism by fire. Interestingly enough, I was not particularly scared at the time. We came under fire several times after that, and all of them seemed to blend into one. However, that first time I remember quite well.

Incidentally, mines were probably the one thing that we all feared the most—especially without close in-shore bombardment. So many destroyers before us had been damaged by mines. My roommate, Ensign Robert Deline, and I always thought that the bow wave would sling the mine out and then bring it back up, hitting us right were we slept in the forward officers' quarters. This thought led to some sleepless nights, but we managed to survive. I will always have a kind spot in my heart for the operators of those little mine sweepers. They would get in close and clear an area, after which the big destroyers would come in and do the shore bombardments and patrols without fear of mines.

Other interesting things I recall about the bomb line in those early days of 1953 was the practice of "H & I." H & I stood for "Harassing and Interdiction" fire. The object was to keep the North Koreans awake and upset by dropping a shell in their laps every ten or fifteen minutes. It probably did keep them awake, but it had the effect of keeping everyone on the USS EVERSOLE awake as well. I remember that Mount 52, the second five-inch/38 from the bow, was right over my head in the forward officers' quarters, so I lay awake many a night as the H & I fire was going off.

To perform the H & I fire properly, the ship had to be travelling at about three or four knots. We would lob shells over to the enemy, and the brass casings for the five-inch/38 would hit the deck. At this slow speed, the ship would roll along rather slowly. The brass casings would roll back and forth, again and again. I hope I will never again hear such a noise as those five-inch/38 casings rolling back and forth on that deck all night long, punctuated every ten or fifteen minutes by a blast. With every blast we knew we had succeeded in keeping the North Koreans awake even longer. The fact that no one on the EVERSOLE got any sleep for five or six days in a row seemed to be of little consequence.

An interesting event occurred after we left the bomb line. We went down off the coast of Okinawa to practice Antisubmarine Warfare (ASW). As part of the ASW exercises, we were required to drop some depth charges to check for leaks in the hull and for practice.

I will never forget an electrician's mate by the name of Rosea. Rosea was from Florida, and his job was to be down in the after steering located right above the rudders, about three decks below the main deck with earphones on during the depth charge crops to detect any leaks that might develop. Somehow the torpedo man set the depth charges to fire too shallow. The result was that the explosion bounced the stern of the ship probably four or five feet up in the air and shook Rosea's gizzard badly. All we could hear on the intercom was cursing and screaming and "What the *&%^%$@ are you guys doing up there?" We all ran back to the fantail and opened up the hatch. There stood Rosea with his earphones half wrapped around his neck, barely able to hold to the microphone. He was the maddest electrician's mate I have ever seen. He had been slightly wounded in an encounter off the coast of Korea while serving on another destroyer, so I suppose loud noises were not new to him.

Probably the most outstanding accomplishment of the EVERSOLE in Korea occurred in late May, 1953. She and the USS KEYES (DD-787) became members of the "Train Busters Club." This organization was dreamed up in the early 1950's for those destroyers credited with destroying a train carrying supplies south from China or North Korea to the communists in South Korea.

There were two main rail lines that ran from North Korea down through the MLR. One went down the East Coast, and the other one was in the center of the country. There were many tunnels through which the trains passed on the east coast line, and ships could blast the tracks all day long only to find them repaired in the morning. It seemed that destroying tracks would do no good.

Our plan, developed by our skipper CDR Victor Delano (the " Old Man" at 34 years of age), was to find a train that was going through a tunnel. After finding the train, it would be a simple matter to seal the tunnel from the front, seal the tunnel from the back, and keep the train inside. Repairing a few tracks was not a major job, but removing an entire train from a tunnel, thus allowing traffic to resume, was a major undertaking.

Each night for several nights in a row we sent over a shore party in the Captain's GIG to listen. When a train went into the tunnel, we sealed the tunnel from both ends, therefore blocking one half of the rail traffic moving south. We did manage to keep one in a tunnel for four or five days, but we were finally sent away on some other task. I can only assume that the train was inevitably removed.

At the time we became members of the Train Busters Club, we were in company with the USS KEYES (DD787). It was late one evening in May. We did hit a train, and we got credit for it. In my service jacket, I used to have a certificate that made me an official member of the Train Busters Club. I have always been proud of that certificate.

Towards the end of the Korean War in June, we went to Hong Kong, and then briefly to Manila. We then returned for a brief period on the bomb line, plane guarding aircraft carriers as I recall. I never will forget when we were detached to return to the States in that summer of 1953. The Commander of the task force, which I believe was Task Force 58, alerted all ships in the groups and sent a special message to DESDIV 31 which consisted of four destroyers: EVERSOLE, KEYES, HIGBEE and SHELTON. The alert was to stand by for a special message for the DESDIV 31 which was being released and sent to the United States, whereupon over the entire network he played the song, "California Here I Come". I never hear that song that I don't have fond memories of that day. The Korean War ended in July of that year. We returned to the States in the summer of 1953. The Korean War ended in July of that year, and that concluded my wartime experiences.

USS *Eversole* DD789
This picture was taken as we passed under the Golden Gate Bridge returning from Korea in June in 1953. Although you can't see me, I am standing mid ship facing just forward of the after smokestack

I also recall an incident that occurred a year or so after the war. It involved a skipper by the name of Robert M. Hill, CDR.USN, one of the finest gentlemen that I have ever known. He was a kind and compassionate man who perhaps did not demand as much of us as he could have.

When Captain Hill was relieved sometime in late 1954, the new skipper was Commander Keith Shortall. It took us all about four days to realize that Captain Shortall was a dictator. He was one of the toughest guys I have ever known! In the After Officers Quarters, where we gathered each afternoon, our vision of life for the next few months appeared very dismal.

After Commander Shortall had been on just a few weeks, Lt. LaCava, who was the executive officer and thus second in command, asked me to go ashore with him to eat supper one evening. I replied, "Yes sir, Mr. LaCava, I will." We went to the Officers Club in Sasebo, Japan. After 30-45 minutes of cocktails, Lt. LaCava asked me, "Blue, why don't you just call me 'Jack'?"

I had enjoyed a couple of drinks by this time, so I thought, "Why not?"

We called each other "Jack" and "Blue" for the rest of the evening. Finally I got up the courage to say, "Jack, for the last year I've addressed you 'Mr. LaCava this' and 'Mr. LaCava that.' Why is it that all of a sudden, here you are just as friendly as can be?"

"Blue, I'm going to tell you something that you should never forget," he said. "On every good ship there is a 'good guy' and a 'bad guy.' When Captain Hill was here, he was the good guy and as number two in command, by default I had to play the bad guy. But as things have worked out, we now have the biggest SOB in the world onboard this ship as skipper. I get to play the good guy for once in my life!"

I have never forgotten that lesson. In fact, it has been one that has served me quite well in my business dealings.

Other Navy personalities that I remember quite well include Ensign Deline, Red Ellis, Steve Hostetler (who is a retired Rear Admiral), Chuck Mann, Jack Deal, Stu Hink, Ben Swan, Bob Cornell, Jerry Wilkerson, Bob Mitchell, Bill Funkhouser, and Ted Burke. Others that I remember are James Eyessel, John Lunsford, Dan Dancey, Joe Chambliss, Dick Ellwood (who used to be a quarterback for the Notre Dame Football team), Mack McCormick, Jack Skomp, Bob Streff, John Witherspoon, Bob Hempel, Roy O'Neal, Arleigh Ronning, and Rusty Reid.

The officer that I remember the most was Sam Purcell, the Chief Engineer whom I relieved. As it happened, Sam was a Mustang who had been at Pearl Harbor during Japan's sneak attack in 1941. He was MM2 at that time, but of course he was commissioned shortly thereafter. Sam was one of the most interesting characters that I have ever known. He married an Australian girl during WWII, and they were living in San Diego during my days aboard the EVERSOLE. After I was released from the Navy, I ventured to San Diego on more than one occasion to visit with Sam. He was one of my dearest friends, as well as a great advisor, counselor, leader, and educator. He has since passed away, but I think about him often.

Although Sam didn't have much of a formal education, he had a certain way of making me learn my lessons. I recall very vividly writing up some work orders to go to the shipyard, whereupon Sam turned to me and said, "Blue, no one can understand that thing; go back and rewrite it." After everything was said and done I must have written work orders for the Engineering Department by the thousands. I learned to describe what I wanted done in very specific terms, instead of my previous orders such as "The generator doesn't work. Fix it." Sam taught me very well.

After Sam left and I became the Chief Engineer, it was my job to take the ship into the shipyard. I required the same specificity of the other officers as Sam had required of me. I was commended very highly by the Chief Engineer of COMCRUDESPAC for the way that we presented our ship to be overhauled.

Obviously, since the Korean Conflict took place from 1950-1953, many of the older officers and the older petty officers had served in WWII. I particularly remember one machinist-made-chief by the name of Bronson. Chief Bronson's destroyer had been hit and sunk during WWII; subsequently, he was captured and forced to spend the remainder of the war in a Japanese POW camp. His POW experience became very significant when we had to go into dry dock in Sasebo, Japan for some rudder repair. Chief Bronson kept looking with a strange expression at one of the dock guards until finally, after two or three days, he turned and he said, "That man was one of my guards while I was in POW camp!" The situation was somewhat tense, as it was not long after WWII and a good many people were still carrying around a great deal of pain.

The story of the way in which our ship was repaired there at the Japanese dry dock remains to be one of the great enigmas of my life. There were two rudders on the EVERSOLE, a port and a starboard one. Each rudder was attached to an approximately twenty foot long shaft that was probably 12 or 14 inches in diameter. Where these shafts went through the hull of the ship, the bearing consisted of lignum-vitae wood in long strips. After a period of time, the strips, which were extremely hard wood, wore the shafts down, so the leakage could not be controlled. Our port shaft began to leak fairly badly while we were in Japan one time, and we had to go into dry dock to get it fixed. You can imagine that pulling a twenty-one foot long, 12-inch diameter steel shaft out of the hull of a ship was a major job. The Japanese cut a hole that was about four feet square into the deck of the fantail. They put up what appeared to be pine saplings and some pulleys and yanked that shaft out, got it over on the dock, rolled it away in dollies, put a collar on it, and brought it back. The entire procedure took about five days. Within less than a week, we were back under way. The other shaft was leaking, but not as badly. When we got back to Long Beach Navy Shipyard that fall, we went into the dry dock to have that shaft and many other parts of the ship repaired. It took the U.S. Navy shipyard seven weeks, with cranes as big as the Empire States Building, or so it seemed, to do the same job that the Japanese had done in less than a week. I remember thinking, "I'm seeing something pretty fabulous and amazing here, but I don't understand what it is." Clearly this was a case of the Japanese making do with what they had. It was a lesson that was lost on me at the time, but I've thought about it many times since.

One of the most interesting incidents that happened to me while in the Engineering Department occurred on the way out of Hong Kong in the summer of 1954. Of course, it was quite hot in those latitudes. One day the starboard engine began to heat up, and after investigating the situation, we discovered that there was no seawater going through the main condenser. Further investigations revealed that the in-take flap was stuck. The problem made it necessary for us to close the mainline and outlet valves and to drain the sea water from the condenser. (The condenser was located along a tube-shaped piece of equipment five feet in diameter and six feet in length.) We had to remove a manhole so that two of us could crawl in and ascertain what was obstructing the in-take flap. One of the machinist mates and I were chosen for the job.

If a person doesn't know what claustrophobia is, he or she should go to the bottom of a ship, one valve away from the ocean, and crawl inside a small tube. Now that's claustrophobia! We discovered that one of the anti-electrolysis zincs had come loose from the hull and had stuck in the flap, thus preventing the flap from opening. The machinist mate and I spent about an hour and a half breaking up the zinc with chisels to work the flap loose. All this work was performed in a temperature of about 105 degrees. Both of us were working in our skivvies.

Probably the worst thing that ever happened to me as engineer occurred in the Far East late in the summer of 1955. I knew at the time that I only had about eight weeks remaining in the service. We were steaming to the United States and were halfway between Pearl and Long Beach, running off of only one of our four boilers and steaming along at about 15 knots. At about midnight, when the crew shifted over to another of our fuel tanks, the engines suddenly went dead. The other ships left us when it became clear that we could not fire off the boiler rapidly. There we were in the middle of the ocean, floating by ourselves.

To make a long story short, at about 0300 we discovered that while taking on fuel in Pearl Harbor, one of the oil kings had left a sluice valve open. When we filled the fuel service tank, we were getting ballast water, but no fuel. When we shifted over to the service tank at midnight, we were trying to burn seawater. Upon discovering the source of the problem, we had just enough steam left on the boiler to turn the blowers on to light off another in the fire room. By 0500 we were back under way. Needless to say, I was not the most popular man on the ship—especially with the skipper.

We went in to the Long Beach naval shipyard that September, and I was discharged in December. As Lt. JG I returned home to Rome, Georgia, and in essence, I have been there ever since. It's funny that as a person gets older, he remembers all of the good things that happened in his life and none of the bad. All in all, I consider my service of two years, ten months, and ten days aboard the USS EVERSOLE as one of the highlights of my life.

Since I left the EVERSOLE I have seen many of my good friends from time to time, even in California and other places. Victor Delano has visited us in Florida and we have met him in Washington. I've seen Ben Swan and Jerry Wilkerson on the West coast several times. In 1999 a reunion of all the EVERSOLE people was held in San Diego, California. Twenty-one of the former officers met there along with about 100 or so enlisted men. In the year 2000, the reunion was held in Jacksonville, Florida where six of the old officers gathered for dinner at our place in Ponte Vedra. One of the more interesting things since I left the ship was in the fall of 1998 when Victor Delano informed me that he found out the EVERSOLE, long since sold to Turkey, was now their national museum ship. Since I was going to be in London for New Years and Christmas of 1998 I decided to go see her. Frank, III flew over the Mary Sue and met me in London the day after Christmas. He and I then boarded a plane and flew to Istanbul. Thanks to my friendship with Will Ball, now president of the National Soft Drink Association, but formerly Secretary of the Navy, we were able to make some outstanding arrangements to visit the ship.

It was sold to Turkey in 1973 and renamed the GAYRET D-357. It was under the command at that time of Captain Salim Dervisoglu. When the ship was retired some four or five years ago, it was decided to make it the National Turkish Museum Ship. I suspect this is because Admiral Dervisoglu is now the top Admiral in the Turkish Navy. In any case, the U.S. Naval Attache from Ankara, Turkey met us and accompanied us to the ship where he had prearranged a visit. We were greeted with open arms. I was presented with a picture of the ship, a baseball cap, and other goodies including a tie. I gave them videos of the ship which I had taken while I had served aboard her. All in all it was a wonderful event and extremely nostalgic to me.

My Experience in Civic Affairs

This is a recounting of those things in civic life in which I have been fortunate enough to have been asked to participate. In essence, it's a story of being in the right place at the right time. Of course, being involved with Coca-Cola helped my involvement more than any particular talent of mine. In the 50's or 60's (and to a certain extent in modern times as well), it was considered one's duty to be involved in civic affairs and to help solve the problems of one's community. To these endeavors was broadly assigned the term "civic duty."

As previously recounted, I was discharged from the Navy in December 1955. I returned to the United States and spent about six weeks in Florida, playing and doing nothing in particular except making the transition from a regimen that was totally foreign to the business world. I came back to Rome in February 1956 and began to work full time. My duties (again, as earlier recounted) consisted mainly of riding routes.

During the spring of 1956, I received my first invitation to join what was considered to be a very prestigious board—the board of the Rome Boys' Club. Mr. Wilson Hardy, founder of Hardy Trust Company (now Hardy Realty Company), called me one day to request that I join the Boys' Club Board. I must preface this account by explaining that Mr. Hardy was one of my great heroes. To offer some estimate of his age, I'll add that he was a letterman on the 1901 Georgia football team. He played the position of end, but I can't imagine that any time in his life he weighed over 125 pounds. He was certainly a feisty fellow-- one of the smartest and most respected men I've ever known.

Despite my utmost respect for Mr. Hardy, however, I did not answer his request immediately. My intention was to buy enough time to enable me to speak with Dad and Alfred to ascertain whether I should involve myself with these sorts of activities or not. At some point in time I informed them of Mr. Hardy's invitation to me, and I must say that the two of them were both extremely good about letting me do what I felt was best. But when Mr. Hardy called me back again a day or two later, I still had not been able to make up my mind. However, the situation soon took care of itself. When he became aware of my still-present indecision, Mr. Hardy announced to me, "Now son, this is something you really ought to do. We'll just count you in." I simply answered, "Yes, sir, Mr. Hardy!"

Of course, it didn't take me very long to realize that sitting on boards and participating in other affairs of this nature provided a very fulfilling pastime for me. The entire decision making process and the opportunity to work with older people whose opinions I respected was a very enjoyable experience. I stayed and served on the Boys' Club Board for about 15 years.

A second opportunity for civic involvement was presented to me in the spring of 1956: Alfred asked me if I would like to join the Rotary Club. In fact, I was very pleased to do so. In those days the Rotary Club met at the Forest Hotel, which was on the other side of Broad Street from the Coca-Cola plant. I was always able to arrive early.

An interesting election occurred in the Rotary Club a year or so after my induction. We were voting for the position of Sergeant at Arms. Now the Sergeant at Arms had to be the lowest and most menial position in the entire club. It was the job of whoever was elected in the position to ensure that the tables were set, the Rotary banner was hung, and everyone was served properly—basically, to make sure that all the behind-the-scenes tasks of the meeting were carried out smoothly. One of my dearest and best friends in the whole world, Al Ledbetter, and I had both joined Rotary at about the same time. The election for Sergeant at Arms—again, I can't overstate how menial the position—was held, and Al and I were both nominated. In those days, the Rotary Club consisted of about 75 or 80 members, and when the votes were tallied, it was discovered that the votes for me outnumbered those for Ledbetter by only one vote. I never found out whose vote was the decisive one, but it certainly wasn't mine. In the end, I accepted the position and served as the Rotary Club's Sergeant at Arms for one year.

The days passed quickly by, and soon afterwards I found myself married to Anne. When she and I married in the summer of 1957, we moved into a house on Sherwood Road, in what is known as "College Park" in West Rome. I had always been, as I remain to this day, a member of First Baptist Church in Rome. Another active member of the church, Dr. Lee Battle, lived up the street from us on Sherwood Road. One evening, he came up to the house after church and asked to spend a few minutes with me. He asked me to become a deacon's assistant (in the church in those days, each deacon had an assistant in his neighborhood to help with the distribution of circulars, with the making of phone calls, and with whatever else might be needed). I agreed. I assisted Dr. Battle for about four years, until he stepped down from the Board of Deacons. When he did so, I was elected to the Board of Deacons in his place, and I served actively for a good many years. Currently, I'm still an ordained Deacon in the church. However, I no longer serve actively.

Little else worthy of mention occurred along the lines of my civic duties during the 50's. In 1958 Frank, III was born followed by Rebekah in 1960. Anne and I then moved to Fieldwood Road because the house we were in was too small. I became very active in the Rome Junior Chamber of Commerce (better known as the Jaycee's). The Jaycee's was a very active club in Rome. Lloyd Summer, Sam Doss, Gardner Wright, and many others whom I've known through the years were all very active members. After I became a member, I was subsequently elected as the club's secretary. Again, it was a menial job that involved a lot of work! As time went on, however, I became less and less involved with the Jaycee's. The two primary causes for my decrease in involvement were 1) I was becoming older, and the Jaycee's was an organization exclusively for men under 35, and 2) the Cartersville Coca-Cola plant had fallen into my jurisdiction, and a great deal of my time was devoted to ensuring that the situation in Carterville was running smoothly. Therefore, in the 60's I had little time to spare with either the Jaycee's or with many of the other civic organizations in Rome.

I did, however, serve as chairman of the United Fund Campaign in the 60's. A gentleman who was president then of Esserman and Company (then the largest and best local clothing store on Broad Street), Jules Levine, had asked me sometime during the late 50's to serve on the United Way Campaign Board. By the early 60's, I was elected as the United Way Annual Fund Board Chairman. Mrs. Hazel Porter, the executive director of the United Fund in those days, and I were prior to that time and remain today to be extremely close friends. She's a wonderful lady who was very helpful to me in my younger days.

By this time I was serving as deacon at First Baptist Church, I had finished a term as the chairman of the United Way Annual Fund, and I had also headed up, along with Mather Payne of WRGA radio station, the Rome Chamber of Commerce Membership Drive. So, in 1961, the Jaycee's decided to name me the Rome Young Man of the Year. I remember very fondly the occasion when it was presented to me. The night the awards were going to be made, and I honestly had no idea I would be the honoree that year. I remember that Anne kept asking me, "Aren't you going to Jaycee's tonight?" And I thought, "What in the world? Is she trying to get rid of me?" She said that my father had mentioned he would like to come to the meeting, and at that point I started to get suspicious because Daddy had never wanted to go to Jaycee's before. My suspicions were well placed, because I did end up being selected that evening as Rome's Young Man of the Year. It was one of the highest honors I have ever received.

Shortly after that evening, I was elected to the board of the Coosa Country Club. What an unpleasant job that was! If a person ever wants to become elected to a Country Club board, he or she should simply complain about the food or go out there on Saturday nights and talk about how bad things are. The first thing you know, friends, you'll be on that board! I served two terms on that board, after which I said to myself, "If I'm nominated, I will not run, and if elected, I will not serve." It was the most thankless task I ever worked at in my life. I did learn one wonderful lesson from the entire situation, though: if a person is not willing to be part of the solution, he or she shouldn't be part of the problem. Complain, and you'll find yourself on the front row trying to solve the problems that you complained about!

The late 1950's and early 1960's seem to have flown by very quickly. Frank and Rebekah were growing up, and as a family we were about to outgrow our little house on Fieldwood Road. Mother and Daddy had decided to build a house next to their house on Horseleg Creek Road. When they did, we moved into the old house. Anne and I still reside in that house at 11 Horseleg Creek Road.

I was in my early 40's then and had attained a small amount of sophistication in serving on boards. It seems that the older crowd was dying out—either that or the boards started running out of bodies. Whatever the reason, I became very active in civic affairs in the 70's.

When Warren Coppege was president of the Rome Chamber of Commerce, an election was held for directors of the chamber. As I remember the story, my father had been elected to the board but refused to serve. He said that his dues to the Chamber of Commerce had been paid. So Warren Coppege suggested that I be appointed in my father's stead. That happened, and I began my service to the Rome Chamber of Commerce. And in 1979 I was asked to serve as president! All in all, I think that's one of the finest services that a person can perform. Everyone ought to support the Chamber of Commerce because of its commitment to making communities better places in which to live.

During the springs of the 1960's, my father, together with Alfred Lee, Harold Clotfelter, Al Ledbetter Sr., and others, always went to Washington D.C. to host what was known as the "Congressional Dinner." Sponsored by the Georgia State Chamber of Commerce, the Congressional Dinner was an event in which two senators and perhaps seven congressmen, together with their respective staff members, were treated to a reception on the occasion of the United States Chamber of Commerce Annual Meeting. Young Al and I would often help to host these annual receptions, allowing us to become acquainted with quite a few senators and their staff members in those days. As a result of the many friendships and associations I made from attending Congressional Dinners, in 1972 I was asked by Pat Patillo (the President of the Georgia State Chamber of Commerce at that time) to serve as the Georgia State Chairman of the Star Student Program. I agreed. In fact, I had been appointed earlier as District Star Student Coordinator by the State Chamber, so the position of State Chairman felt relatively natural for me to accept. My service with the Star Student Program was essentially my first move into anything like a state job. I remember being thrilled to death because I knew that being State Chairman of the Star Student Program meant I would serve a term on the State Chamber

Board, which has always been a highly prestigious position.

    As it happened, the man who preceded me as State Chairman of the Star Student Program was Bill Jones, whose family owned the Sea Island Corporation. Bill was, and to this day remains, a very close friend of mine. He called me one day to say, "Frank, I've got a real problem. I've been accepted to Harvard Graduate School, which means that I've got to be in Boston during the Annual Star Student Program Meeting over which I am to preside. Will you take my place?" I agreed, and in effect the result was that I served as Chairman. It was a great service and one I enjoyed extremely. One of the things that happened during the State Star Student Program was on a given Saturday night in the spring, WSB channel 2's television station televised the proceedings Live. The highlight of which, I as Chairman was to introduce the Senior U. S. Senator Herman Talmadge for his address and the presentation of the awards. I had known Senator Talmadge for a good many years so I was not at all apprehensive about this and in fact was looking forward to it. I had my little introduction prepared which Anne made me run thorough in the kitchen several times to be sure I had it correct. As we were rehearsing, my tongue slipped and I said the senior citizen Herman Talmadge. From that point on the nervousness began and I started thinking, oh my goodness I am going to introduce him as the senior citizen and not the Senior Senator. I'll never forget at the time when the occasion came I remember standing at the podium and looking down at Anne when I came to the words and I said very deliberately, "Senior Senator". She almost broke into an audible laugh with relief. It was a great service and one I enjoyed extremely.

    After my service to the Star Student Program, I was fortunate enough to be re-elected as a full fledge board member of the State Chamber Board. I was elected President of the State Chamber of Commerce in 1980.

Among the other events of the 1970's was my invitation by Lam Hardman II to join the Georgia Baptist Foundation Board. (Lam, who lived in Commerce, Georgia, was my mother's first cousin. He was a great gentleman who died prematurely on a military trade mission in OS Sweden. His children, Lam III, along with Dr. John Hardman and daughter, Shell Knox, remain to this good day my very close friends.) I served for two terms, one from 1972-75 and one from 1977-82. I also served as president from 1978-82. The Georgian Baptist Foundation was an institution that had been founded back in the 1940's. In those days, the funds given to statewide Baptist causes, such as the Georgia Children's Home, the Georgia Baptist Hospital, Shorter College, and Truett-McConnell College, were maintained separately by independent boards, or, in some instances, by local churches. It occurred to several active Baptist business people in those days that the funds were not being administered in the most effective way possible. Thus, they formed the Georgia Baptist Foundation (GBF). The GBF requested that the boards of the individual Baptist institutions each place their funds in a common pool, so that the interest and earnings would be distributed but not the principle. The idea was a controversial one and was, in many cases, not well received. However, in retrospect, it seems that the founders of the GBF were taking a very sensible initiative.

The Appalachian Health Systems Agency (Appalachian HSA) was another organization I served during the mid to late 1970's. Conceived by Lyndon Johnson during his term as United States President, the Appalachian HSA was one of Johnson's many "Great Society" programs. The purpose of the Appalachian HSA was to help control medical costs—it might seem a somewhat impossible task today, but the popular thought in those days was that such a goal could be achieved successfully. The Health Systems Agency covered between 12 and 14 counties in North Georgia, from Gainesville to Dalton to Rome and in between. Here's the way the program worked during the time in which I served: if a hospital in Dalton, for example, wanted to buy an MRI machine or some other such expensive piece of medical equipment, the hospital would contact Appalachian HSA and request permission for a Certificate of Need, known as a "CON." The Agency's board, which during my service consisted of 40-50 members, would then study the issue at hand. Meeting quarterly at various locations throughout the state, we would make final decisions on where to distribute the agency's funds.

The difficult thing about decisions to distribute funds was that certain hospitals had a tendency to join forces to push other hospitals out of the picture. This was certainly the case with Dalton, Gainesville, and Rome. If Dalton's hospital needed an MRI machine, for example, and we determined that we could only afford to send two to that region, Dalton and Gainesville would vote for each other to gang up on Rome. Added to the difficulty was that Rome had two hospitals, Floyd Medical Center and Redmond Park Hospital, that feuded all the time and kept Rome from accruing a strong vote. Dalton and Gainesville won every time. It was a totally political solution to an economic problem—it was just a very bad situation. In any case, I served on the board of Appalachian HSA for several years. Subsequently, the agency was dissolved.

I was asked to serve on the HSA Board through my association with Redmond Park Hospital, a private hospital owned by the Hospital Corporation of America. Dr. Tom Frist, Sr., who was then President of the Hospital Corporation of America, in Nashville, Tennessee, joined with several other active Rome citizens to build a private hospital in Rome. Dr. Lee Battle was elected as the first Chairman of the Board. He subsequently asked me to join the HSA Board as its first lay member—a request to which I readily agreed. My acceptance of the position was in no small part due to my belief that competition (in the medical field as well as in the world of business) creates a much better situation for everyone involved.

Upon the opening in 1972 of Redmond Park Hospital, a building that was considered then to be a modern marvel, a series of long lasting disagreements began to transpire between Redmond and the local public hospital, Floyd Medical Center. The competition between the two was acrimonious, to say the least.

I remember one particularly interesting incident that occurred. The two administrators of Redmond and Floyd, Ed Tinnerman and Ben Ansley, respectively, were the two main persons responsible for fomenting the discord. Ben Ansley was a former military hospital administrator and a retired army colonel. He and Ed clashed upon sight. As each of them stirred up their respective boards about what the other hospital was doing, the situation was magnified. Finally, someone suggested that a joint meeting between the two boards be held one evening at the local Holiday Inn (located on the banks of the Oostanaula River). Both boards agreed that it would be an excellent way of thrashing out problems and resolving some of the difficulties. The administrators thought it was a wonderful idea as well, but I think that they each had visions of gladiators standing on the sidelines, urging their troops into battle!

I remember the cocktail party and dinner with great detail. It soon became apparent to everyone that although the two boards were enemies in theory, the reality was that the members of the boards knew each other all too well! For example, Billy Maddox, who was chairman of a particularly powerful committee on Floyd Medical Center's Board, was also president of National City Bank. Among the members of National City Bank's board were Tom Watters and myself, both members of Redmond Park's Board! Many of the other individuals there at the banquet found themselves in similar circumstances. Needless to say, the two boards quickly began to intermingle. The funniest part was to watch Ed and Ben sitting there together. Instead of watching their two boards clash, Ed and Ben watched their board members discuss their other mutual interests! I'm not sure that those two gentlemen completely learned their lesson, but they certainly got the message that the two boards were not going to fight and that everyone had a sense of community and cooperation at heart. I'm happy to report that the feud cooled down considerably after that evening.

In addition to my involvement in the medical field, I also became involved with some activities in the field of education. My first foray into the educational field occurred in the 1970's, when I was asked to join the board of Thornwood School. The school had been formed in the early 1960's by a group of Rome leaders—principally Dr. William Harbin, Al Briley, Vernon Grizzard, and Harold Story—and was housed then as it is today in the old Colonel Shorter house on Shorter Avenue. Located on the corner of Shorter and Horseleg Creek Road, the school was situated right up the road from where I live presently. The purpose of Thornwood was to found a type of sister school to the all-male Darlington School, with the intention of offering a tougher intellectual challenge to those girls in Rome who might desire it. Approximately two or three years after the formation of Thornwood, I was asked to join the school's board, and I did so gladly. I served as a member until Thornwood merged with Darlington in the late 1970's. Therein lies a tale.

In the early 1970's—1974 as I recall—a fairly severe recession occurred in the United States. Times were rather tough. The recession lasted approximately 18 months, and as the recovery started back, Darlington became concerned about a few of the social changes that were going on in the world. For example, Darlington's boarding school enrollment began to diminish. As a result, the Darlington Board began to consider the possibility of admitting girls. In a similar situation to that of Rome's two hospital boards, many of the members on Darlington's board were married or strongly acquainted with members of Thornwood's board, and vice-versa. Naturally, we all began to discuss the option of merging Darlington and Thornwood together into one school. Some feelings of bitterness did emerge, understandably, because many of the Thornwood girls and their parents didn't want to give up Rome's only all-female school. Being a product of all male schools myself, I could very easily sympathize with their frustrations. However, it appeared that Darlington was serious enough that if the two schools were not to have merged, then Darlington would simply have begun accepting girls. After several years, Darlington would have inevitably posed a significant threat to Thornwood's student base. Thornwood was finished either way you looked at it.

Darlington and Thornwood merged together in the early 1970's, and the entire Thornwood Board became Darlington Board members. I served on the Darlington Board some years after the merge. Later, I was to serve again, and presently, I am once more serving as a Darlington Board Member.

At this point in my life, my involvement with the Rotary Club again became significant. As previously recounted, I had served in the late 50's as Sergeant at Arms of the Rotary Club. As the years passed, I was subsequently elected to the Board of Directors and served more than one term in the directorships of some of the various vocational avenues. In 1976, I was asked to become President of the Rotary Club, and of course I accepted this great honor and challenge.

I remember from those days a particular member of the Rotary Club named John Rooney. He was a great friend of mine. John worked at Hardy Realty Company and was also a devout Rotarian. Much of his civic life revolved around the fact that he was so interested in Rotary. In fact, he had served as president of our club. Whenever John Rooney would be travelling throughout Georgia and would refer to someone back in Rome, he had a certain way of saying, "You know, he's a past president of Rotary Club." But the way he said it, the phrase "past president of Rotary Club" became one single word—"pastpresidentofRotaryClub." I always found this expression very funny—that is, until I served as President. Then I realized that being "pastpresidentofRotaryClub" was the best thing a fellow could hope for, and that the quicker I got out of that position the happier I would be. It was a great service, but it was very time consuming. The weekly concerns of preparing the programs, assuring that dues were paid, and responding to the members' complaints what to do about programs (and especially food!) made the president's job a very busy one. Of course, despite everything, I remain of the opinion that the Rotary Club was and remains one of the finest civic organizations going. I admire anyone who agrees to serve as a president of that organization.

Among my other attempts at service in those days include my membership on the Georgia Council on Economic Education (GCEE). For several years I served on the board of that organization, which was designed to promote economic education in high schools. I also served on the Georgia Foundation of Independent Colleges Board, which was an organization dedicated to raising money for 12 private institutions throughout the state. Because Rome was home to two such institutions, Shorter and Berry, these schools probably received a disproportionate amount of funds. The board provided an excellent initiative for maintaining high quality private institutions and colleges.

In addition to my service on the boards of the Georgia Council on Economic Education and the Georgia Foundation of Independent Colleges, I also served on board the Floyd County Airport

Commission. The way that I became involved in the organization was this: in the mid 1970's, Mike, Al, Alfred, and I purchased a corporate airplane and built a hangar out at the airport. We hired a full-time pilot so that we could use the plane whenever we needed to run back and forth between Rome, Valdosta, Fort Valley, and Carrollton. Subsequently, the airport began to be the cause of various political arguments—something involving the Floyd County Commissioners who failed to understand the importance of aviation and those commissioners who saw the airport as a great tool. The Airport Commission was soon implemented as a go-between these two groups.

The Airport Commission turned out to be a very successful organization because it relieved the County Commissioners from personally having to investigate how an airport was run. The economics of an airport are very confusing. Some of the commissioners thought that exorbitant fees ought to be charged for use of the airport. However, the county had no cost basis in the facilities because the Navy had donated the airport—completely built, paved, and ready to go—to Floyd County upon the completion of World War II. But somehow, due to the application of modern accounting principles, a very large depreciation sum was held against the Airport Commission's bank account. It made our operation look terrible. Though I had been a member since the commission was originally formed, and eventually served as Vice Chairman, I subsequently went off the board. I have always held, and maintain to this day, the opinion that the airport could be one of Rome's economic assets if it were to be developed properly. Today, the Airport Commission is operating very successfully as far as I know.

In 1971, a very significant event occurred to me. I was asked to join Berry School's Board of Trustees. John Betrand, who was then serving as Berry's President, and Harold Clotfelter (President of Hardy Realty and one of Rome's all-time leading citizens), came to ask me one day if I would complete the term of John Maddox (a very fine lawyer in Rome who had recently died prematurely). I certainly agreed to join their board. To this good day I remain as a board member, and in this coming January I will have served for 28 years. I have probably served on all the committees at some time or another: I've been Chairman of the Oak Hill Committee, Chairman of the Executive Committee, and now I'm back as Chairman of the Oak Hill Committee once more. I have seen Berry go from an $8 million a year budget to $40 million one. The endowment has grown from under $100 million to over $300 million dollars. Berry College is a wonderful institution, and my service on its board has been a commitment of which I am extremely proud.

Me, William Chesney Martin, former Chairman of the Federal Reserve Board, and Bill Bowden, President of Trust Company Associates at Berry during the Inaguration of Dr. Gloria Shatto, April 19, 1980

Another major event that occurred to me the early 1970's was that I was asked to join the board of National City Bank. My father had turned 70 in the fall of 1968, and according to the bylaws of the organization, at that time he was required to retire. The board requested that I assume his position. I ended up serving on the board of National City Bank from 1969 until 1986 or 1987. In that time, I saw the bank go from deposits of under $40 million to amounts so large I don't even remember them. Many other major changes occurred during that time as well. My brother-in-law, Lloyd Summer, served for many years as a very successful president, and he helped the bank grow to be a major contributor to the economic success of Northwest Georgia. Under the directorship of such wonderful leaders as Lloyd, Billy Camp, Tom Watters, June Todd, Billy Maddox, and others, National City Bank at its height held something close to 65% of the deposits in Rome and Floyd County.

In the early 1980's, Lloyd was approached by a

One of the things you have to do occasionally is get involved in politics. I enjoyed being Chairman of Sam Nunn's committee for re-election in Floyd County.

good friend of his and mine, Charlie Presley, to join some ten other banks throughout the state in forming a statewide banking system. (Charlie was president of the Georgia Railroad Bank in Augusta.) It turned out to be a very successful project. In effect, our bank merged with Georgia Railroad, allowing us to receive Georgia Railroad stock in exchange for our National City Bank stock. This step up at that time was considerable. Some four or five years after we had merged with Georgia Railroad, however, First Union absorbed the Georgia Railroad Institution. I remained on the board for four or five years after that, but subsequently I elected to resign as we had sold our business and I no longer felt the need to serve on a banking board. However, I must add that the step up in value that our stocks received by all of the mergers was most rewarding.

As you can see, the 1970's were an extremely active time for me in civic affairs. The 1980's began a new era; my father had passed away, Alfred Lee was getting on up in years, and I had turned fifty. While I hate to think of it this way, I had become what might be called "a seasoned old pro in all things civic." My children were both in college, and I began to think they might even graduate from college and make something of themselves! In other words, I was beginning to settle into middle age fairly comfortably.

The 1980's brought an invitation for me to become even more involved in state politics. A basic tenet of the Coca-Cola business, which I had been raised to believe, was that a person had better get involved in politics if he or she wanted to have any say so in governmental control of business. As previously indicated, Daddy and Alfred believed in this theory wholeheartedly, having both been active in the Georgia Chamber of Commerce. I had been active in State Chamber of Commerce work—involvement in politics always felt perfectly natural to me. I had been involved in the election campaign of Carl Sanders, George Busby, and many others.

In the early 1980's, I became very much involved in the election campaign of Joe Frank Harris. Of course, Joe Frank had been a friend of mine in Cartersville for many years. He was elected as Governor of Georgia and immediately put me to work. The first thing Joe Frank asked me to do was to join a board that he had created, called "The Governor's Consumer Advisory Board." I served on that board for two years. The board's purpose was to advise people about false advertising, truth in advertising, and other matters involving consumer product complaints.

Joe Frank Harris wants to be Governor and he did!
1982

Perhaps a good way to describe the new board would be to say that we were a "watch dog" committee. At the first meeting, I was asked to become chairman—an honor that I accepted. Our first job was to fire the current Consumer Advisory Board Commissioner; fortunately, though, he resigned before we had to take such drastic action. Subsequently, we hired Barry Reid for the position. He has been the board's Commissioner ever since.

After a year or so on the Consumer Advisory Board, I was asked to join the board of the Georgia Department of Trade and Tourism (Georgia DITT), a board upon which I served for 14 years. We served as the State of Georgia's marketing arm for industrial growth. As Daddy, Alfred, and I had been involved in industrial development in Rome and Floyd County, I felt very comfortable in my position on the Georgia DITT Board. George Berry was the board's commissioner at that time; I served with him for about six years until Randy Cardoza was appointed as the DITT Commissioner in his stead. Randy remained the Commissioner until just recently. I believe that my service on the Georgia DITT Board was among the most entertaining—as well as productive—jobs that I have ever had.

1982 was a very busy year for me. I was on the NSDA Board, an active member of the DITT Board, a past president of the Rome Chamber of Commerce, and a member of the Consumer Advisory Commission—among other boards. Then, in 1982, I was asked to become President of the State Chamber of Commerce. It soon became apparent to me that participation in these various civic activities had less to do with ability than it had to do with being in the right place at the right time. If a person were somewhat visible in the community and knew folks around the state, and if a spot on a particular board were to be vacant in the area in which that person lived, then chances were pretty good that he or she would be a prime candidate for the job. The board members might say to each other, "Well, old Barron lives up in Northwest Georgia, and he's a nice fellow. Let's just pick him." I rather suspect that I was asked to join so many state boards just because the board needed a member from Rome and someone on the board knew me.

Later in the 1980's, I was asked to join the Board of the Chieftain's Museum. (Then, the Chieftain Home was known as the John Ridge Home. It was located in the Celanese community.) I served on that board for several years. I also served on the board of The Peanut Factory, which was a fledgling peanut manufacturing company started by Charles Clotfelter. The Peanut Factory was a wonderful organization that did very well, only falling into hard times very recently. I served on that board for a good many years as well—until we sold our Coca-Cola business. My lawyers advised me at that time to resign from as many boards as possible, which I did.

In 1983, I was asked by my good friend Joe LaBoon, the president of Atlanta Gas Light Company, to join the Atlanta Gas Light Board of Directors. (When Joe had been in Rome as the Regional Vice-President of Atlanta Gas Light, he and I had become fast friends. Our friendship grew when I followed Joe as President of the Georgia State Chamber.) I readily agreed to serve, and in fact I remain a member of the board to this good day. I have found it to be a most fascinating experience. During my service as a board member, the gas company was listed on the New York Stock Exchange. Today due to the help of a great many wonderful presidents such as Joe LaBoon, Dave Jones, Walt Higgins and most recently Paula Rosput, the gas company has grown into a very successful company. All in all, it has been an experience that I value very much.

Also in 1983, Anne's first cousin, Tom Watters, died tragically from a heart attack at the age of 53. He left behind him five young sons: Tom, who was in his middle to late twenties; Bill, who was just younger than Tom; and the other three boys, who were not of working age. He a left behind him a large, very successful company, Integrated Products, which was a mill that spun yarn to the specifications of the carpet industry and sold the yarn to make the tuft of carpets. Tom had willed control of the company to three individuals: Billy Camp, Grover Maxwell, and myself. But we were not in control of running the company per se; perhaps it would be more accurate to say that we were made into a board of directors took care of the basics and allowed other events to run their natural course. We decided in the end to appoint young Tom in charge of the business (he was 27 or 28 at the time). I have never had reason to regret our decision. Tom, his brother Bill, and now Thad and Joe who later came into the business, did a simply marvelous job of managing it before the business was sold to a group in Memphis. They later started a business called Syntex and have been very successful in that as well. They are fine young men. The youngest boy Ed, went into the Landscape Design business. He also has a huge yard maintenance service. When Anne wanted to hire him, I said you better be careful because my Daddy used to say, never hire anybody you can't fire. Anne said, I'm not worried about his performance, if he messes up I'll just call Helen, his Mother.

    The 1980's were very busy years for me as a Rotarian. I was made a "Will Watt" Fellow, which is an educational sort of award. In 1984, I was asked to serve as chairman of a committee to raise funds for the commissioning ceremony of the U.S. Georgia. That in itself is a very interesting story.

    Nuclear submarines built by the U.S. Boatworks in Groton, Connecticut are named after states, such as Virginia or Washington. The SSBN729, or the "USS Georgia," was one of 15 or 20 ballistic nuclear missile submarine that had been launched by the Navy. These ships were huge! When each submarine was commissioned (that is, officially given to the Navy by the U.S. Boatworks), the state for which the boat had been named was expected to host a sizable reception. Our committee's duty was to raise the funds for this reception. In the end, I recall that our efforts brought in about $15,000-$20,000!

Anne and I were very fortunate in learning how to prepare for such a large event. The year previous to the commission of the U.S.S. Georgia, the U.S.S. Florida (another nuclear submarine) was commissioned in Tallahassee. Anne and I were invited to attend the reception and to educate ourselves on the hosting of such a tremendous event. It was a most interesting occasion. We were lucky enough to meet the Governor of Florida, who readily explained to us what needed to be done.

The year quickly passed, and before long we found ourselves making last minute preparations for the commissioning of our state submarine. Soon, it was the day of the ceremony. The Georgia National Guard flew at least 200 guests—including Joe Frank Harris, who was the governor at the time, and Mac Mattingly, who was the Republican Senator from Georgia—from Georgia to Washington D.C. to attend the event. Anne, Rebekah, and I flew up on our company plane. We invited Dr. John Bertrand, who had been awarded a Navy Cross during World War II for heroic activities while aboard a submarine (and who also happened to be President of Berry College at the time), Jimmy Dick Maddox, who had also served on a submarine during World War II, and their wives to fly along with us. We attended the three-day ceremony and a large dance held in honor of the State of Georgia. We even entertained the captain of the Blue Crew and the Gold Crew one night at dinner. During the ceremony on the day of the commissioning, Senator Mattingly delivered the keynote address. Governor Harris, Anne, Rebekah, Pete (our pilot), and I were honored to receive a private tour of the submarine after the reception was over. All in all, it was a most enjoyable experience.

In the early 1980's, Governor Harris created a commission called "The Growth Strategies Commission." Its purpose was to predict and prepare for Georgia's future needs. In the 18 months that the commission was in session, all possible fields of Georgia's future were explored—from the environment, to transportation, to taxes, no stone was left unturned. A gentleman who is presently serving as president of the Georgia Conservancy, John Sibley, was named executive director of the project. (A highly talented lawyer, John was the son of John Sibley I and the younger brother of Jimmy Sibley. The Sibleys are a very distinguished Georgia family.) Joel Cowen, whose close acquaintanceship with Governor Harris probably stemmed from the fact that Cowen's father had served as the mayor of Cartersville for several years, was named chairman. The fact that I was appointed to this important committee came as a great surprise to me.

    I was sitting in my office one day after having been out of town on business when I received an urgent phone call from Gracie Philips, Governor Harris' appointment secretary. Now, the term "appointment secretary" always sounded to me as though it was Gracie's job to arrange the Governor's daily schedule, but the truth of the matter is that Gracie was the person in charge of securing final appointments for the Governor's various boards and committees. She and her husband, Barry, a lawyer in Atlanta, have long been very dear friends of mine. Anyway, Gracie called me on the phone one day to say, "Frank, I've been trying to get in touch with you for days!" I, of course, was totally surprised. When I inquired about the purpose of her call, she declared to me, "Get ready, because you've been appointed to the Growth Strategies Commission!" I had been aware that the commission was of being appointed, but it certainly never occurred to me that I might be place on the committee. Gracie explained to me, "I've been trying to catch you for a week, but I just couldn't find you. I just said to the Governor, 'Go ahead and put Frank's name on the list; he'll do it!" and the Governor said, 'Okay.' So I hope that's all right!" Of course, the appointment was more than all right with me. I was simply thrilled and delighted!

For the most part, our meetings with the Growth Strategies Commission were very probing and intensive. The commission members were from a variety of backgrounds—business, education, and the environment, to name a few—so that as many viewpoints as possible would be represented. I was placed on the Environmental Committee. Milton Bevington was the chairman of this particular committee, and Roy Barnes, as well as many other notable Georgians, were fellow members along with me. (When I say "notable Georgians," I don't mean by any stretch of the imagination to include myself in this category. Many of the people I was privileged to work alongside were, however, quite extraordinary individuals.) As a group we made many useful recommendations, and as an entire board we produced a legislative package that in the end was almost totally adopted. That legislation is still in effect to this day.

One club I was asked to join in 1981 was the Gridiron Secret Society at the University of Georgia. I had studied Thomas Carlisle's book, Sartor Resartus, and found myself inducted into Gridiron in November of 1981. I consider membership in that great society to be one of the highest honors a Georgian can ever achieve.

The Human Relations Commission was another initiative launched by Governor Harris. Created in December of 1987, the commission was formed in response to some race riots that had occurred down in Forsyth County. As one can well imagine, Georgia became the object of some extremely negative criticism as a result of these riots. We were nearing the end of the 1980's, and Southern states simply weren't supposed to have race problems of such magnitude. Governor Harris immediately suspected that these events could lead to some serious problems. Thus, his thought was to create a new governmental commission, with representative from males, females, and as many racial and cultural backgrounds as possible so that we could attempt to solve such problems before they exploded.

Governor Harris' new commission became known as "The Humans Relations Commission." It was chaired by Felker Ward, a black lawyer in Atlanta who subsequently became a very close friend (in fact, he and I serve today on the Atlanta Gas Light Company Board). Other members of the board included a rabbi, some Catholic laypersons, and an Indian representative. We had Hispanics; we had Blacks. We had every single racial possibility that one might imagine. At one of our retreats, I found myself admitting to the group, "You guys, I suppose everyone here should consider me to be the token white Anglo-Saxon Republican in the group, because I don't know what I'm doing here and I have no idea how to solve all these problems!"

During my time on board the Human Relations Commission, we attended some extremely interesting lectures and study groups that taught us a great deal about the multi-faceted world of prejudice. I learned more about the perceptions of prejudice than I ever thought possible. Hopefully, I came out of the experience a much more open-minded person. I resigned from that board after about two years, however, because I soon perceived that the group was becoming more and more proactive. In my opinion, "pro-activity" is often just another word for "interfering." When we went out in public, we seemed to lose all impartiality, which in turn made us out to be very ineffective. The group did go into the communities and attempt to set up local human relations committees, and as far as I know, those committees are presently doing very well. Despite its shortcomings, the group was served by a great many marvelous human beings. I still see and hear from many of them to this good day.

In the mid to late 1980's, an extremely significant honor was bestowed upon me: I was asked to serve on the Carter Center Advisory Board. After his defeat by Reagan in 1980, Jimmy Carter elected to build a library, as most presidents do. The Carter Center Advisory Board was founded to assist in the leadership of this library. It was, and remains to this day, a very prestigious board. One might imagine my excitement when Mr. Carter asked me to join! During his political career, I had not been a very strong supporter of Carter. However, I have since become convinced that his activities as a former President have been quite miraculous. He has probably been the most effective ex-President this country has ever known.

Although in the late 1980's (the time of the board's founding) the Carter Center Advisory Board members were asked to serve indefinite terms, the structure of the organization changed a bit when Dr. John Hardman came to serve as executive director. He reconstituted the board in such a way that a multitude of individuals were requested to serve. The terms were necessarily limited so that more people would have a chance to become involved, and in the process, a number of the original members were given the honorary title of "Lifetime Member." President and Mrs. Carter were asked, of course, and I was extremely honored to have been asked. I hold my position as "Honorary Lifetime Member of the Carter Advisory Board" to be one of the highest honors I have ever been given. I serve as a lifetime member on that board to this day.

On June 30, 1986, we sold our bottling companies, and from that point on, my life changed rather dramatically. I went from getting up at 5:15 every morning—starting the day with the Coca-Cola Company and staying at work until at least 6:00 every night—to a much more relaxed sort of day. I could come in later in the mornings to write letters, make phone calls, and do other sorts of activities necessary for my involvement in civic affairs. Karen, my secretary from the Coke plant, was gracious enough to come along with me to my new office after we closed the plant. She remains with me to this day and is a wonderful help.

As the 1980's gave way to the 1990's, I resigned from some of the boards to which I was no longer a great help and joined others to which I hoped in some small way to contribute.

In addition, around that time I was asked to serve on the University of Georgia's Foundation Board. Tom Cousins, a longtime friend of mine who grew up with me in Rome, became President of the University of Georgia Foundation and immediately began to make several changes. He expanded the Foundation Board and asked me to serve as a non-University of Georgia graduate, which I did. I served on that board for six years.

In the year 1991, as I recall, three very significant things happened in my life. First, Anne's mother passed away. Our son Frank had been activated as commanding officer of a local reserve army unit and was sent to spend seven months in Saudi Arabia during the Gulf War. It is my opinion that this is what finally made him decide to become a commercial pilot. When he returned from the Gulf War he came to me and said, "Pop, I'm sure you would like for me to go in business but I've been sitting over there for seven months thinking about. All I really want to do is fly airplanes." I told him it's a rare person at his age that not only knows what he wants to do but has the ability to do it and to go for it. I don't know anybody who is happier in his work than he is. Third—an event to which I would like to devote some attention here—I was elected as President of the Georgia State Chamber of Commerce—again.

In 1991, the Georgia State Chamber of Commerce (which had been renamed "The Business Council of Georgia" when it merged with the Georgia Business and Industry Association) was doing very well. However, for some reason, the board decided to make some changes in the person of the executive director. The title "executive director" had changed by this time to that of "president" and the lay leader was the "chairman of the board." In any event, Gene Dyson, the current president, was asked to leave. (He went on to serve as interim president of the U.S. Red Cross and now owns a consulting firm.) In September of 1991, I received a phone call from Walt Sessoms, the Senior Vice-President of Bell South Company, who also happened to be the Chairman of the State Chamber. Walt explained the situation to me and asked if I would serve as president on an interim basis while the committee conducted a search. My term was estimated to last approximately 60-90 days, and all that I was really requested to do was to go down to Atlanta once a week, sign a few checks, and tend to the office until a new president could be found. I readily agreed to help.

When the vacancy was announced, there were at least 130 applicants who called in immediately to request the job! After about six weeks it became readily apparent that the search was going to take far, far longer than anyone had anticipated. Under the direction of Pat Pittard, the local director of a worldwide executive search firm named Heidrich and Struggles, we began a nationwide search. Soon, I realized that I was going to have to spend a lot of time in Atlanta, so Anne and I decided to rent an apartment there. We enjoyed it so much! (In fact, we loved being in Atlanta so much that soon afterwards we bought a condominium there, which we keep and maintain to this day.)

In the middle of this entire situation, I decided to call up my lawyer, Charlie Shaw. I said, "Charlie, as you've probably heard, I'm down in Atlanta running the Georgia Chamber. Does pro bono mean what I think it does?" He laughed and said, "Yes, it does. You're driving that bus for free!" But I have never regretted that experience for a single day. I never had more fun in all my life, and that's the truth!

One interesting aftermath of the Chamber thing occurred in that next year. A group of lobbyist had formed themselves together to form the Golden Pigeon Club. Golden was reference to the golden dome on the Georgia State Capitol and Pigeon referred to what lobbyist did to the Capitol. It was all in great fun. After my year at the State Chamber they made me an honorary Golden Pigeon and I have a small plaque testifying to that. It was a great honor and one I treasure.

I received a great honor by the Leadership Georgia Board of Trustees in the early 1990's when they named me a J.W. Fannin Fellow. This was an extremely special award created by the board. Then, in 1991, Governor Zell Miller made me an honorary admiral of the Georgia Navy. One might ask, "Even though a person had been a former destroyer officer, what in the world would they do as an admiral in the Georgia Navy?" My answer would be very straightforward and simple: "I'll be damned if I know!" Nonetheless, I received a certificate announcing I had been named an "Honorary Admiral of the Georgia Navy." Of course, I was very proud to have been so honored.

Thanks to my wife Anne, I was named a Paul Harris Fellow by the Rotary Club the mid-1990s. Soon afterwards, in May of 1994, Washington & Lee honored me by electing me to membership in ODK, which is a leadership fraternity. I have continued my association with Coca-Cola for all these years and have been named Vice-President of the Rome Coca-Cola Bottling Company. I am proud to say that I still hold that title.

In addition to serving on the Berry Board of Trustees, Atlanta Gas Light, and several other boards, I also served on the Richard B. Russell Foundation Board. The Richard B. Russell Foundation was formed soon after the death of Georgia's then Senior, Richard

B. Russell. Dick Russell, as he was called, was one of the most honorable and revered citizens in the State of Georgia and even in the United States. He was strongly considered as presidential material at one time but this never came about. The Foundation was formed with proceeds from his estate to form in the University of Georgia Library, a sub-library called the Richard B. Russell Library. This was to house not only his papers but the papers of other famous Georgians who have held high government offices. Already in this library at this time are Governor Lamartine G. Hardman's (previously mentioned as my Great Uncle), Governor Zell Miller, many congressmen, and the collection grows daily

Another major committee that I have served on is the Georgia Research Alliance. Perhaps I should say a few words about this particular board. The Georgia Research Alliance (GRA) was created by leaders throughout the state as an attempt to consolidate the sizable funds that the University System of Georgia was spending on research. The idea was first put forth by Governor Harris during his administration in the early 1980's, but nothing materialized from the idea at that time. Several of the university presidents saw the alliance as a threat to their school budgets, while others viewed it as a piece of pork barrel legislation that would not stop until it got to Athens. And so nothing happened.

However, later in the 1990's, the business leaders of Atlanta became quite upset at the money they saw being wasted. They looked to other states, such as Texas, California, and Ohio, as being the technical leaders of the country, while they saw Georgia as lagging further and further behind. Several business leaders joined forces and hired McKinsey and Company, a (a nation-wide consulting company) to research what Georgia might do to improve its industrial future. The results were that we needed to spend heavily on telecommunications, the environmental sciences, and biotechnology.

Based on these three initiatives, the Georgia Research Alliance was formed. It consisted of six or eight business leaders throughout the state, as well as the presidents of the six major Georgia institutions of higher learning: Emory University, Clark College, The University of Georgia, The Medical College of Georgia, The Georgia Institute of Technology, and Georgia State University. I was asked to join the board as I had served as a past president of the Georgia Chamber of Commerce and as a member of the Georgia Department of Industry, Trade, and Tourism. Under Governor Zell Miller's leadership, when the alliance was formed we began to allocate around $18,000,000 per year towards the hiring of eminent scholars in the three critical need areas.

Since that time in the early 1990's, something in excess of $240,000,000 has been allocated to these six major research universities to hire eminent scholars. The goal, of course, has been economic growth—to develop those sciences so that the citizenry of Georgia could compete with anyone else. On more than one occasion I have announced to Bill Todd, the first and current leader of the Research Alliance, "When all is said and done, I will probably be able to say that my service on the Research Alliance has had more long term effect for the state of Georgia than any of my other activities." I served on the committee for six years before my term expired. To this day it remains a most effective organization.

Other boards on which I have served recently include the Board of Trustees of the Georgia Public Policy Foundation, the Board of Visitors of the Emory University Foundation, and the Richard B. Russell Foundation Board. I was also asked several years ago to serve on the Advisory Board of the Georgia Conservancy, which I serve on to this day. I also served as Honorary Chairman on the Annual Fundraising Campaign. Additionally, three years ago I was invited by Mike Egan and others to join the Trust for Public Land Board, which is a board dedicated to buying lands from the private sector and then turning them over to the State Government, the Federal Government, or certain trusts. A prime example of the board's activities would be its recent attempt to acquire lands bordering the Chattahoochee River, all the way from Lake Lanier to Atlanta, for conservation purposes. It is truly a wonderful organization.

My hobbies though the years have included a fairly reasonable interest in University of Georgia football, although sports in general are not a chief interest of mine. I never was a golfer or a tennis player. I suppose my current hobbies include a deep and abiding interest in music; in addition, I am a consummate reader. I do attempt to play the piano to some degree; I enjoy playing for 30-40 minutes every night. I don't play for anything except for my own entertainment—it is particularly entertaining when one makes as many mistakes as I do. I would consider myself an active scuba diver, as at least once a year I go off with several men and spend three of four days of intensive scuba diving. I have a small Cherokee 140 airplane that I probably fly for about 30 hours a year. My flight is purely recreational—a fast bicycle rider could probably outrun that little airplane! If you're trying to get anywhere in a hurry, my airplane is not going to take you! My idea of a perfect way to start the day is to fly for an hour or so, early on Sunday mornings when it's crisp in the fall, so that I can savor the colors of the mountains with someone who enjoys it as well as I do.

Now and then I am asked to take on additional civic activities, and I suppose one might say that the boards I serve could be considered my hobbies as well. I presently serve on the Board of Trustees of Darlington School, the Richard B. Russell Foundation, the Georgia State Chamber of Commerce, the Atlanta Gas Light Resources, Berry College, the Carter Center, Georgia Public Policy Foundation, the Trust for Public Land, and the Board of Advisors for the Georgia Conservancy. I remain a somewhat active member of the Rotary Club and, of course, I still hold memberships in ODK and the University of Georgia Gridiron Secret Society.

One of the fun things I was asked to do recently was to serve as the Honorary Maestro of the Rome Symphony Orchestra. As a teenager, I played a baritone horn in the Rome Symphony. When they asked me to be the Honorary Maestro for a fundraising campaign I was thrilled. I led a jazz band at their fundraising kickoff party. When I told them I wanted to wear jeans they came up with the idea to have the men to wear jeans and tux jackets and shirts. Everyone loved it and a great time was had by all.

There are many other odds and ends of public service in which my family and I have been involved. My father's accomplishments and those of Alfred Lee are so numerous that I could not begin to try to enumerate them. One thing that I would like to mention about my father is that in the late 1980's, he was inducted into the National Soft Drink Hall of Fame. This was an extremely high honor. He also, as far as I know, is one of the very few (if not the only person) to hold an honorary lifetime membership on the Board of the Coca-Cola Bottlers' Association. My mother privately held the honorary title as President of the Coca-Cola Bottlers' Association Auxiliary for many years. She would preside at dinner meetings and would have a lot of fun making everyone laugh. She was very good at that.

Anne, my wife, was asked to join the Horchow Family Board of Advisors in recent years. She has served very graciously and effectively as a board member for several years. I managed to go to one of the annual meetings with her in Dallas. It was great fun being "Mr. Anne Barron." She also has served for several years on the Board of Advisors for the Southeastern Flower Show.

Rebekah began to show signs of leadership in her young years when she was asked to become one of five travelling Phi Mu sorority representatives immediately after she graduated from college. She spent a year after college travelling all over the United States. She has just been asked to serve on the State Board of the Girl Scouts. We are, of course, very proud of her.

I've already mentioned Frank's participation in the Gulf War. He is now employed as a captain with Atlantic Southeast Airlines, which is a subsidiary of Delta Airlines. He has flown with them for seven years now. My son-in-law Joe Montgomery has also done extremely well for himself. Since he has been in Rome he has been elected to and attended the entire course of Leadership Georgia. He has just been elected Chair-Elect of the Georgia Conservancy which is a very prestigious job in the state. He is presently serving as Vice-President of College Affairs of Shorter College and has done extremely well there. Of course, I am extremely proud of the accomplishments of all my family.

Mary Sue Barron (Susie) – She was a bird in her day

Potpourri

In reading all that I have written, various odd and sundry incidents occur to me which are not connected either with my civic life, the Navy, or the Coca-Cola business. For example, one of the most pervasive things in a man's life are the homes in which he lives. It might be of some passing interesting to my grandchildren where "Pie" and I lived all these years.

When Anne and I first married in 1957, we lived in a very small home on 212 Sherwood Road. We bought it from Steve and Joyce Smith. Steve is a local pediatrician and a very close friend. His family and our family have been friends for many, many years. We lived in that small house for over three years, but when Rebekah came along it was apparent that the house was not big enough for both Rebekah and Frank, who had been born two years earlier. We then moved to 8 Fieldwood Road. We lived there for 8 years, from 1962 to 1970. After that, we moved to 11 Horseleg Creek Road, where we presently live.

The house at Horseleg Creek Road has a right interesting background. It was built in about 1927 by Mr. Poundstone, from Atlanta who was quite an architect in his day. He built the house where the Shorter College President now lives, known as "High Acres," and also the house where Bob Ledbetter now lives. The houses were all built around 1927 or 1928.

Our house on Horseleg Creek Road was originally built for Mr. Calder Willingham. The Willingham family name is an old and venerated name in Rome history. Calder did many interesting things through the years, including running and operating the Third Avenue Hotel. He had three children, two of whom I knew fairly well. The older son, Caulder, Jr., was a very famous author who died in 1997. Among other things he wrote the screenplay to the movie, The Graduate. He also wrote a book called Rambling Rose.

Rambling Rose was the story of a maid who came to work for the Willingham's in the late 1920's and early 1930's when they lived at Horseleg Creek Road. Rose was quite a character, but she is best described in the book. The book was made into a movie in the early 1990's and was a serious contender for an Oscar. However, it never won the award. The movie was about a young boy growing up and being nurtured (in more ways than one) by his maid Rose. In any case, many of the places that were mentioned in the book are familiar to me. For example, the secret room in the book was well known to me when I was growing up. I think even by now my grandchildren have discovered it. Certainly Frank and Rebekah knew about it.

After Mr. Willingham built the house in 1927, he sold it sometime in the mid 1930's to Julian Morrison, the supervisor of the mill in Shannon. Mr. Morrison sold it to my mother and father in 1940. They lived in the house until 1970, when they built a new house right next door. Later, Burgett Mooney moved into the house next door, and Anne and I moved into my parents' previous home. We live there to this day.

In addition to my home, Ponte Vedra Beach, Florida has long been an important part of my life. When I was about 5 or 6, I vaguely remember going to Atlantic Beach in the summer and staying at the old Clarkson Cottage. Then, in the late 1930's, my father bought a house in Ponte Vedra from a man named Frank Rogers.

Mr. Rogers and his brother-in-law, Jim Stockton, had developed Ponte Vedra in the late 1920's and early 1930's. My father owned that house until about 1940, and I remember it fairly well. In 1940 he, my Uncle Alfred, and my Aunt Kathleen built a house right up the road again on the beach in Ponte Vedra.

I can remember very clearly being in that home during WWII times. I remember my mother having to draw the blackout curtains at night. In those days, the Coast Guard patrolled the beaches because there was great fear of invasion. If a person left one single window cracked, the Coast Guard would come knock on the door and request that the lights be cut off or the curtains be rearranged. Also I remember the Coast Guard patrolling the beach at night on horseback looking for alleged saboteurs. Airplanes flew over at all hours, and Navy Blimps even went up and down the beach looking for what I suppose to have been submarines.

A book was written about sinking ships off the coast of Florida, North and South Carolina during the early days of WWII. It was entitled <u>Operation Drumbeat</u>, and it was written by a former German submarine commander. My mother used to describe very vividly seeing a submarine sink a ship off the coast of Ponte Vedra in about 1942 or 1943. She and all the folks on the beach got up and watched the shells fly by from the submarine and hit the ship, which then caught on fire and sunk. She used to tell the story about the honeymoon couple that was staying at the Ponte Vedra Inn. The bridegroom had enjoyed several drinks before deciding that the thing for him to do was to get into one of the lifeboats and paddle out to rescue the sailors from the sunken ship. Unfortunately, the current took him south, and he was picked up by a freighter, deposited in Cuba. The gentleman didn't get back in the United States for six weeks.

In 1949, my Father and Mother sold their interest in the house in Ponte Vedra, and for two years we had no house in Florida. Virginia and Lloyd were living in New Orleans and Virginia Beach. Lloyd had been recalled back to the Navy and of course, they were never able to go. I was in college, and it looked like the Florida days were behind us. My Father couldn't stand it. He bought a house in 1951 at 565 Ponte Vedra Boulevard. This house is presently owned by my children, Frank and Rebekah. In 1990, after looking around at all the children and grandchildren that were coming along, Anne and I decided the thing for us to do was to buy another house. We did so, and we presently own a home at 525 Ponte Vedra Boulevard.

The house in Ellijay is another house that we own. It's just a cabin in the woods. When Anne and I were much younger, we used to do a fair amount of white water canoeing along with Scott and Nan Henson, Lam and Mary Hardman and others. One day we paddled the Cartecay River in Ellijay, and I remember thinking that if I could ever find a lot on that river, I would certainly like to build a little cabin up there. By this time, I was in my early 50's and the children were in college. My financial worries were beginning to diminish.

I was at the Dalton Coca-Cola plant one day when I saw an ad in the local magazine advertising riverfront lots on the Cartecay River. I excused myself from the business of the day and drove straight to Ellijay right then. Two weeks later Anne and I bought a lot. This was in February, as I recall, and we spent the first night in the house on July 5th of that same year. The house was built very quickly. We've expanded the house in Ellijay a little bit since then, and of course we are still enjoying it.

In addition to our homes in Florida and Ellijay, Anne and I also maintain a condominium in Atlanta. That home, however, is mostly in our possession because of my involvement with the Georgia Chamber of Commerce in the late 1980's and early 1990's. But that is another story. It does appear, however, that the Atlanta investment has turned out to be a good one because Joe and Frank and Rebekah use the condominium all the time.

Another house that played a large part in my life in my youth which has not been mentioned before, is the house on Mount Alto. In the mid 30's, Daddy and Uncle Alfred decided to build a retreat to have political parties, barbecues and the like. They bought a small lot up at the juncture at Radio Springs Road and Mount Alto Road, some seven miles to the West of

Rome on down Horseleg Creek Road. They built a large cabin. It had four bedrooms upstairs and a sleeping porch. Downstairs was a single bedroom and a huge fireplace which dominated the great room. The great room took up nearly all the first floor. All during my college days, I can remember spending my weekends up there with Martin Turbidy, Fred Malone and others. Towards the end of the early 50's they decided to sell it inasmuch as it was being broken into on a fairly regular basis. Later it was owned by the Hackett family and was known as the "Hack Shack". I understand there were some fine parties in those days but I was not part of that.

I have been blessed all my life with good and interesting friends. Some of them have been real characters. Of course, I could not mention "characters" that I know in clear conscience without referring to Kiki Petropole. Kiki's full name was Angelique Pete Petropole, but she was known and loved by all of us simply as "Kiki." Kiki was a fairly large girl, although the word "large" may be an understatement. She was my age, and we grew up and attended grammar school together. Kiki went to a convent for her undergraduate school and then went into nursing. She was Dr. Harlan Starr's nurse during most of his years in practice. Harlan, of course, was our pediatrician. Kiki could be as sweet as anybody as you ever saw, and also as mean as a hornet. She was present in the delivery room with Anne when Frank and Rebekah were born. In fact, while in labor Anne announced, "I'm not having this baby until Kiki gets here." And she didn't. We probably spent more time talking to Kiki on the telephone when the children were young and growing up about illnesses than we did with Harlan. But I'm sure that suited him, and it certainly suited us.

As Kiki got older, she remained a very close friend. I can eating some of her wonderful dishes both at her house and at our house in Ellijay, Ponte Vedra and Rome. Kiki was a fabulous cook. She eventually published a series of television shows based on her culinary prowess. All in all, Kiki was a marvelous woman. She was a wonderful dancer and was very light on her feet for such a large woman. She also had a beautiful voice and appeared in all the local follies. Kiki was always one of the stars.

Kiki did have her moments, however. She had diabetes, and in the latter years of her life she became somewhat incapacitated. I was named executor of her will and was given power of attorney to pay all her bills. As good as Kiki was and as smart as she was, Kiki had come from a fairly affluent family. As a result, she had problems handling money. She didn't look after her finances as well as she should have, and she tended to be somewhat of a spendthrift. My job was to keep Kiki from spending herself into bankruptcy. As a result, I would control her credit cards, pay all of her bills, and chastise her when she overspent her budget.

As I mentioned before, Kiki had somewhat of a volatile personality. One of my favorite stories has to do with the time she called me one day after I wouldn't allow her to make a particular purchase. She called my secretary Karen and in a very loud voice screamed, "Is his Royal Asshole there?" Without any hesitation Karen said, "Just a minute Kiki, I'll get him." I heard the conversation and went running into Karen's office. I told Karen she could have at least asked Kiki who had been talking about! We have laughed many times over that particular incident. My grandchildren probably don't know it, but when they were younger we used to go to the Country Club for Sunday lunch, and Kiki would say, "Here comes the Beauty Brigade!" She always referred to the little girls as the "Beauty Brigade." I always loved that.

Kiki died tragically of a massive heart attack in 1992. We have all missed her. To this day, Anne still has such brief thoughts as, "You know, I need to know how to cook a certain item. I'll just call Kiki. She'll know." Kiki was truly a wonderful person and a very special part of our lives. We still miss her.

A particular pastime that I have enjoyed increasingly since my retirement is traveling. The first time I ever ventured outside the United States, other than the brief trips to Canada because of my Aunt Kathleen, was when I was in the military. I saw Asia, Japan, China, and many other places in the Far East.

After my military experiences, I decided that I would like to see Europe. The first trip Anne and I made that was of any consequence was at Christmas of 1972. We decided to take the children on a trip sponsored by the Coca-Cola Bottlers Association to Majorca, Spain. Majorca is an island located in the middle of the Mediterranean Sea. We flew there on Christmas afternoon and stayed for one week. The trip must have stimulated our interest because it seems that we have not looked back since. I have always felt that a week or two in Europe or some other part of the world is probably as good of an education as a young person might ever receive. In later years, Anne and I traveled to France and Germany on some other Coca-Cola trips, but none of the trips lasted over a few days.

After our Coca-Cola business was sold in 1986, I not only had more time to travel. But I also had a little pocket change. The first major trip that I took with my children was what Frank and Rebekah and their spouses refer to as "The Grand Tour." We flew to England where we stayed a few days. Anne and I then went to France where we met Frank and Trisha and Joe and Rebekah. From there, we embarked on a three day balloon trip over and around the Loire Valley. It was a trip put on by the Buddy Bombard group. After three days of ballooning, we went to Paris to board the Orient Express, travelling to Venice for three days and then coming home.

Since our "Grand Tour" to Europe, Anne and I have been to Ireland, England, and Italy with the children. The deal that I've made with them is that I'll fly them over and back and put them up for two or three days, but after that they're on their own. Our travels have been very rewarding experiences that I have enjoyed as much as the children. The past two or three trips, some or all of the grandchildren have gone with us. I have had so much fun watching the little girls begin to expand and learn what other countries are like. They've begun to come to the realization that if a person doesn't understand the international markets, they're just not going to be in the twenty-first century. Aside from that, our travels have given me some awfully good food, some awfully good wine, and some awfully good times.

One of the places where I learned as much as anything else I've ever done occurred when I served for fourteen years on the Georgia Department of Industry, Trade and Tourism Board. During my service, we were privileged to go on several overseas trips. I went to France, Germany, Italy and Canada. The political clout that was held by the DITT was such that we were able to have receptions and meetings with political powers of the country or community where we went. We were exposed to fairly intensive briefings by leaders in the European Community. In France on one occasion, we met with the head of the France's Economic Department. He was also Governor of the Region of Lorraine (which is somewhat akin to being a Governor).

After several years on board the DITT, a person comes to understand that the United States does not stand alone and there are not big walls around our country to protect us. It had been hoped that we'd perhaps learn this at the end of WWII, but there are those who think we can remain isolated. When I saw how fast other countries are developing and the amount of economic and intellectual expertise that abounds in these countries, I realized that our only hope for survival is to be as good as or as better than the other countries are. I suppose this is the underlying reason that I have always felt it so valuable to take the children and grandchildren to Europe, so that they can see for themselves what other countries are like. The idea has been pointed out much more eloquently than I have that we are not in competition with some fellow from Alabama or some fellow from California. We are in competition with the bright kid from Seoul, Korea or some brilliant young scientist from France. All in all, the world is becoming a much smaller place. We must be prepared to deal with that reality.

Fishing

Among the other trips that I do manage to take from time to time involve going on a group fishing trip at least once a year. This all started back in 1963. In that year, Tully Roe asked me if I would join a fishing trip to Homosassa, Florida that had been taking place since the early 1930's. I accepted the invitation gratefully. At that time I was, by all odds, the youngest of a group of about 12 or 14 people. As time has passed, the group still continues but now I'm the oldest of the group. We've been going to Apalachicola for thirty some odd years now. Also, a group of us has taken an annual scuba diving trip somewhere in the Caribbean in the past 25 years. We've been to such places as Belize, Aruba, Curacao, and many other places too numerous to mention. This next year, 2001, we are going to Stella Maris, Bahamas.

Canoeing

At this point I'd like to relate the story of how we came to venture to the Okefenokee Swamp once a year. The Okefenokee Swamp is one of the most significant natural marvels in the United States. Its over 400 thousand acres of swamp land are a magnificent nature laboratory. Twenty-five years ago, when I discovered that there were canoe trips available for people who wanted tour the swamp on a self-guided tour, I decided that was the thing for me to do. Six of us, Scott Henson, young Scott, Jo Stegall, young Joe, Frank III, and me decided that we would go. The boys were all 15 at that time. We received permission and had a reservation to paddle into a place called Craven's Hammock. It was an 11 mile paddle in and an 11 mile paddle out. We planned to camp that night on the island of Craven's Hammock.

We planned the trip for six weeks in advance. We'd meet once a week, talk about the menus, tents, clothes, etc. The first trip was so successful that we decided to make it an annual trip. Eventually, we branched out. All the girls go with us now, and we're even taking our grandchildren. It's a marvelous canoe trip we take once a year. The last couple of years we have been to Joe Montgomery's family place on the Suwanee River. Instead of spending a night on an island somewhere, we paddle some of the pristine rivers of Florida, including the Ichatucknee, Santa Fe, Suwanee, Wacissa and others. We will go again this year.

Real Estate

There are some interesting things that happened in the past relating to real estate developments. Sometime in the late 1940's, my Father, Barry Wright, Al Ledbetter, Sr., Knox Wyatt, Wilson Hardy, Harold Clotfelter and one or two others decided to start a real estate company. Of course, the main purpose of the company was to make a profit, but another of the group's goals was the economic growth of Rome and Floyd County. The men formed a corporation called the Echota Corporation. It's a land development company that probably founded to build the old Sears Roebuck Building, located on Second Avenue across from Central Plaza in Rome.

As time passed, the philosophy of creating small, highly leveraged real estate corporations to build buildings, lease them, and create assets seemed to be working. Subsequently the owners of the corporation (which grew to include Al Ledbetter, Jr. and myself as time went on) formed several more corporations. One of these was Shorter Realty, created to build some buildings for Integrated Products, Tom Watter's company. Another one was NCB Development Company, created to build another textile plant.

One of the techniques in these corporations was to use the money of an SBA, or Small Business Act, to construct these buildings. A requirement of the act was that the company has at least 25 stockholders. Many publicly minded citizens joined in these corporations, most of which have now been sold or otherwise disposed of. Echota and Shorter Corporations are still viable businesses. There are very many stockholders in these companies now because the children, grandchildren, and in some cases great-grandchildren of the founders are now the stockholders. They're interesting corporations that have grown to be fairly large and extensive in nature.

South American Adventure

For time immorial, people have thought of a pot of gold which is at the end of the rainbow. This quest for gold and jewelry has never stopped, and I myself have not been immune.

Clint Provost, a friend of mine who went to Darlington with Al Ledbetter and me, appeared on the scene one day looking for investors in a treasure junket. The basis of the whole scheme was that Clint, a precocious scuba diver, had discovered through some research papers a gentleman in Ecuador. This particular gentleman had found the lost treasure of Anhuatapec, a legendary Incan Chief. In order to hide his gold, Anhuatapec had supposedly dug a cave, hid his gold, and then built a dam at the end of the gorge in which the cave was located. He filled up the gorge and built a lake, thus submerging the cave underwater.

According to Clint (who, by the way, was a master salesman), Anhuatapec's lake was located up in the Andes some 60 or 70 miles from Quito, the capitol of Ecuador. Clint needed a few investors, so he enlisted Tom Selman, Julian Reese, Al Ledbetter, Penn Nixon, I, and several others to put money in this venture. The amount of money put by each of us was at this time a fairly enormous amount. As I recall, we each contributed $250.

After one or two trips to Quito on our money, Clint came back and said only one more investment would be necessary. However, by this time some of the investors had decided they didn't want to contribute anything else. Al Ledbetter, Penn Nixon, and I remained hooked. By this time, the Atlanta Journal and Constitution had gotten wind of the trek and was preparing to write a big article about the trip.

One night, Penn and Al decided to submit to Clint's request that we go to Quito and see how our venture was coming along. They asked me if I would go, but I refused. Late one Tuesday night about 8:30, they called and said, "We're leaving in about 3 hours and flying to Atlanta on the Ledbetter company plane. We will then catch a plane to Panama City and go from there into Quito. We'll stay two days and come back. Are you sure you don't want to go?" At the time they called me, it seems that I had drunk a martini or so. I decided, "What the heck, why not?"

I ran to the Coca-Cola plant quickly, got my passport, and called them back with the news that I was ready to go. Penn and Al assured they had called Delta and that the tickets were available. I was in on the deal. We went to the airport and flew from Atlanta, to Panama City, Panama thence to Quito.

When we arrived in Ecuador, we were unable to find Clint inasmuch as he was "out in the field." We were taken by one of Clint's friends to listen to an alleged radio transmission from Clint, talking about how he was "just almost" on the track of the gold. This was very exciting and very heady stuff. As we finished our two day stay in Quito and were on our way to the airport, Al and Penn informed me there was just one minor hitch. They had been unable to secure a return ticket for me, so I would probably be unable to travel home on the same plane as them. To make a long story short, I actually bribed the ticket agent and was able to get on the same plane. I still have the newspaper clippings of our venture in my files. Of course, nothing ever came of the gold, and Clint died an untimely death some years later. It was fun while it lasted.

Flying

For many years, I have been interested in flying. When I was a teenager in high school I started flying at the Richard B. Russell Airport in Rome. One of my first instructors was a native Roman by the name of Jimmy Best. Jimmy was a friend of mine of long standing and was my sister's age. Jimmy soloed me on September 19, 1950. This year I have been flying for 50 years. I discontinued shortly after college because I had the Navy to consider, and after that I didn't have any money.

In 1977, as mentioned earlier, we bought a fairly sophisticated airplane. Mike, Al and I were running all over the state in cars and literally trying to kill ourselves in automobiles. As I said, Pete held an instructor's certificate, so it seemed only natural that I should start flying again. Shortly after that, my cousin Mike started flying as well. He and I together bought a 1967 Piper Cherokee 140. As time passed, Mike got another plane and things changed. Mike sold his share of the Cherokee to me. By this time Frank III was flying, and so I sold him Mike's half of the Cherokee. Frank subsequently upgraded, and I became again the sole owner of the Cherokee which I have to this day. It's a very pristine airplane and in excellent shape. I still fly it as often as possible but not near as much as I'd like.

The company later traded in the Cessna 421 for a King Air C-90. Towards the end of our time at the Coca-Cola plant, we upgraded to a King Air B-100. This was a large 10 seat airplane and was really more than we probably needed. When we sold the business in 1986 of course that airplane went with it. All that is left is my little Cherokee.

Manson Family Scare

Sometime the early fall of 1975 I was in my office one morning about 10:30 when I received a phone call from The Atlanta Constitution in Atlanta, Georgia, asking me what I knew about the Manson family threat to kill my Father. Immediately of course I answered I knew nothing of the subject. I thought at the time that the man was a quack but he kept on talking and sounded authentic and said there has just come over the wire a press release from some radio station in New Orleans listing 1200 people that had been identified as targets by the Manson family. You may recall the Manson family killers were a notorious California group who wantonly murdered some people and were apprehended and sent to jail. There was a young lady by the name of Squeaky Fromme who was involved in this incident (it may be recalled that she was the one who attempted to kill President Ford). In any case, there were three Georgians named on this list. A gentleman named Gray who was with General Electric Company and a William Barron who we presumed to be my father. I was loathe to think it was me but it may well have been since we shared the same name. In any event after talking to the gentleman from the Constitution for a few minutes I realized he was not kidding and he was certainly for real. I said at the time "Sir, I don't think I better talk to you anymore. I need to find out about this." and we discontinued the conversation. I then called the local FBI office and asked if they had information or was this some quack call. The agent in charge said he didn't know what I was talking about and he had no information about this and he would call me if he heard anything. He said you told me your name is Barron is that correct? I said yes, that's correct. He said wait a minute, my partner is waving his hands at me. He put me on hold. He came back on the phone and said Mr. Barron there is defiantly something to this, where is your office. I told him and he said we'll be there in 30 minutes. I said fine, thank you. I of course was tremendously alarmed at this. I got hold of my uncle and my two cousins Mike and Al and told them the story as I knew it which was 15 minutes old. I then called my brother-in-law who was President of the local bank half a block away and said "Lloyd, you better get up here. We've got a problem." We all met in the conference room with the two FBI agents who had learned a great deal more and indicated there is absolutely something to this. There has been a list released, we don't know how authentic it is but we certainly do not take these matters lightly. We treat them as real threats and we intend to take this one in that way. At this point my uncle said, "Do you think we should arm ourselves?" and the FBI agent said we cannot under any circumstances tell you to do that but if it were me and I were being threatened I would certainly do it. Alfred said, "Mike run in there into the office and bring out some pistols." Alfred kept a small safe in his office which he kept 4 or 5 rifles and maybe 15 or 20 pistols. He walked back in the conference room with 8 or 10 pistols and said, Frank would you like to keep this one, this is a good little 32 and said Lloyd how about you? Lloyd said, now I've got a 45 that I've had for years, and so on and so forth. One of the FBI agents said you know, I think they've picked on the wrong crowd this time. Nothing ever came of it but there was an enormous amount of newspaper and radio publicity over the next several days from Atlanta and all over the Southeast. As a matter of fact about the three Georgians as well as many other people across the United States. It was a very juicy news story. We were advised by the FBI and also by the Coca-Cola Company security people to vary our driving habits and our shopping habits, etc. so as not to create a pattern. The great fear was not that the Manson family would indeed attack us but that some crazy out of Atlanta would try to get his name in the newspaper by doing something silly. The company paid for personal guards for each of our homes for six to eight weeks after that point in time. At the end of the eight weeks the story had died down and nothing ever came of it but it was an exciting time!

The four "Rebekahs"

Easter 1996 in DITT shirts. Front row: Anne, Mary Beth and Hannah Montgomery and Emily Barron. Back row: Anne Barron, Mary Sue Barron and Me.

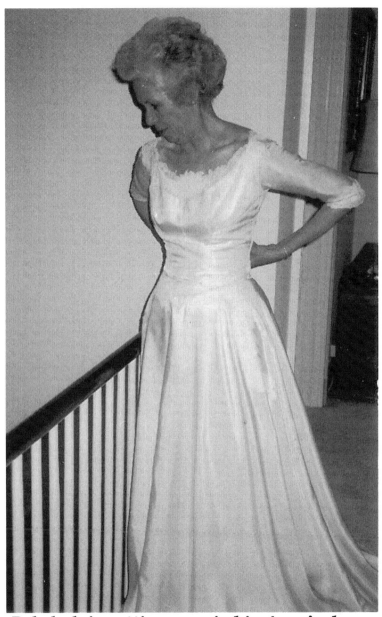

*Rebekah is getting married in Anne's dress
–and it still fits Anne! 1984*

Susie, Anne Montgomery and Mary Sue Barron –1987

Susie and Mary Sue

Rebekah and Frank, III at Rebekah's wedding in 1984. In the background is a portrait of Rebekah when she was 16.

This is Frank, III and Rebekah at age 4 and 2.

Vanessa Mosley. She helped write this book.

Afterward

This sums up my life as far as it's gone so far. Since the original writing of this, I have had a heart catherization which discovered a small blockage. It was treated with angioplasty but at the present time I'm not able to fly. I am going to attempt in 6 to 9 months to see if I can't get recertified.

Not much else has changed dramatically in my life.

Afterward in Retrospect

Since writing this book, several things have happened. First, I have had my physical which resulted in my being recertified to fly. I have retired from the boards of Atlanta Gas Light Company, Berry College, Darlington School, and Century Bank of Cartersville. All of this is a result of turning 70. In the thanks which I expressed in my **Memorandum of Thanks**, I referred to an "unknown typist from Berry College." As fate would have it, she was Natalie Miller, now Natalie Ferguson. I have been working very closely with her as she is the auditor of the Century Bank of Cartersville upon which board I sat. I also was named Darlington School Distinguished Alumni of 2001.

-Frank Barron, February 2002

3rd Afterword

Since the last printing of this book, in 2002, life has gone on. I have bought a new airplane, an LSA Light Sport Aircraft. Picture is below. Nothing else has changed, family is doing well. I was honored by receiving the Northwest Georgia Council Boy Scouts Distinguished Citizen award in 2010. In 2012, I was awarded the Leadership Georgia "H.G. Pat Pattillo" Award. In September 2012, my college, Washington and Lee University, honored me as a distinguished alumni. Other than this, life is progressing.

I also want to thank Mary White, a student at Berry College. She had the task of transferring all the book data from floppy disks to CD. I will always be grateful to her.

-Frank Barron, August 2013

Mary White

Memorandum of Thanks

I cannot let the opportunity pass without thanking those people who are most responsible for this book. First, I must thank my son Frank, III and my son-in-law, Joe Montgomery for goading me into doing this. They would hear me tell stories of the Coca-Cola business and the early days of Willie, my Father and others. After insisting for several years that I, somehow or another, write down these memories or else they would be gone forever with my passing. I did sit down and filled up eight voice dictated tapes. As near as I recall it added up to over seven hours of dictation. It has boiled down to this final document.

Secondly, I must thank an unknown typist from Berry College who did the first rough draft. The great debt for this document in its present form belongs to Vanessa Mosley from Dalton. She was a senior at Berry College when she started working on this document and now she is teaching school in Dalton. That is an idea of how much it has taken. Vanessa has consistently revised, renovated, challenged, corrected and polished this endeavor. To her belongs a tremendous degree of thanks.

Of course much of the final polishing was done by Karen Stinson, my faithful secretary. She has done an outstanding job of drawing it together at the end and making me continue these revisions.

Brian Charbonneau of the Rome Printing has been most helpful in guiding us in how to go about putting this in some sort of book form. I don't think we could have done it without him.

The final proof reading was done by my wife, Anne Barron. She found many corrections of dates, times and events. Above all she kept me from getting too full of myself in this whole thing.

Thanks to all the above.